KARMA
AND
REINCARNATION

KARMA
AND
REINCARNATION

The Key to Spiritual Evolution and
Enlightenment

Dr HIROSHI MOTOYAMA

Edited and translated by Rande Brown Ouchi

PIATKUS

© 1992 Hiroshi Motoyama

First published in 1992 by
Judy Piatkus (Publishers) Ltd of
5 Windmill Street, London W1P 1HF

Reprinted 1994, 1996

This edition 1998

Reprinted 1999

**The moral right of the author
has been asserted**

*A catalogue record for this book is
available from the British Library*

ISBN 0-7499-1916-7

Set in 11/12½pt Linotron Baskerville by
Computerset, Harmondsworth
Printed and bound in Great Britain by
Biddles Ltd, Guildford and King's Lynn

CONTENTS

EDITOR'S INTRODUCTION

This book is a compilation of writings on karma and reincarnation published in Japanese by Dr Hiroshi Motoyama over the past 15 years. The body of the text is loosely based on two written sources, *Rinne Tensei no Himitsu* (The Mystery of Transmigration, 1981), which I translated from the original Japanese, and the monograph 'Analysing Individual Karma and Reincarnation', published by his research institute in 1986. These texts, in turn, are largely comprised of edited transcripts of lectures given by Dr Motoyama to his many students and to Shinto followers. This turned out to be a bit problematic when preparing for an English edition because of the great number of shared philosophical assumptions between speaker and audience. In working with the material, I have tried to weave as many of these assumptions into the text as possible, in order to give the work a more comprehensive and definitive context. The 'hidden' material comes from years of discussion and correspondence with Dr Motoyama and his staff and they, of course, have carefully approved this final version.

There are two larger contextual issues, however, that I wish to address in this introduction. The first, about the author; the second about how the material was obtained.

Dr Motoyama is an unusually gifted and learned man who is difficult to categorize. His areas of expertise span many disciplines. He is both a man of science and of religion: a priest, a philosopher, a yogi, a physiological psychologist, a computer specialist, a researcher of oriental medicine, a parapsychologist who trained with Rhine in the 1960s, an electrical engineer, a spiritual healer and a seer.

He was born in 1925 on the island of Shodoshima in the Seto Inland Sea in Japan. Dr Motoyama began his spiritual training when he was five years old under unusual circumstances. His natural mother, Seiko Yoshima, is by nature a deeply religious woman. While on a spiritual pilgrimage with her young son, she met the founder of the Tamamitsu Sect of Shintoism, Reverend Kinue Motoyama (Odaisama). Reverend Motoyama was a profound mystic and healer who had recently experienced revelations of the upcoming war (World War II), and had been directed to establish a Shrine on Shodoshima and a congregation devoted to the cause of world peace. When Reverend Motoyama met Seiko Yoshima and her son, she realized that their three destinies were tightly interlinked. She intuitively understood that the woman was to be her spiritual companion in her life's work and that the boy was to be her spiritual successor. Seiko Yoshima reciprocally felt such a deep affinity and trust in Reverend Motoyama that she and her infant son soon joined Reverend Motoyama on a pilgrimage throughout southern Japan, praying for peace at various Shrines.

The two women immediately began to instruct the child in forms of spiritual practice and asceticism that normally would be initiated when a child was much older, such as the traditional rite of chanting sutras while standing almost naked under a freezing waterfall. But the boy responded ardently, and soon began to have experiences of the non-physical dimensions of existence – 'mystical' or 'spiritual' or 'religious' experiences. He began to have regular experiences of clairvoyance and telepathy, and was able to communicate with disembodied spirits in the higher dimension. He was very aware of the presence of the Divine principle functioning in the material world.

The three of them eventually settled permanently in Tokyo, where they established a branch of the Tamamitsu Shrine in 1935. The boy (Dr Motoyama) began a daily regime of early morning yogic exercises, prayer and meditation in his teens. He attained major spiritual breakthroughs in his twenties. Reverend Motoyama adopted him as her successor, and the three remained together until Reverend Motoyama died in 1974. Seiko Yoshima, now aged 85, continues in the position of Head Priestess of the Shrine, where Dr Motoyama is the Head Priest. Dr Motoyama and his mother faithfully continue to broaden and deepen their experiences of the nature of reality through daily practice.

Dr Motoyama was an exceptionally brilliant student. He began his academic life as a philosopher with the professional aim of assessing the nature of spiritual experience in a logical, objective manner. He obtained his PhD in Philosophy and Psychophysiology in 1962. He gradually became frustrated by the inability of philosophy to communicate or bring about the direct experience of higher states of consciousness. Around the same time, he became aware that his 'mental' experiences were creating physiological changes in his body. He began the study of psychophysiology and medicine in order to ascertain what those changes were, to try and begin to apply the rigours of modern scientific discipline to objectify the process of the evolution of human consciousness. To this aim, Dr Motoyama founded the Institute of Religious Psychology in 1960, a bustling research facility located in the grounds of the Tamamitsu Shrine.

Years of physiological research on many individuals who had undergone similar spiritual experience (Indian Yogis, Zen masters, psychic surgeons from the Philippines, Catholic healers, etc.) led him to speculate that the mind and body are connected through a subtle system of energy circulation not yet recognized by Western science. He speculated that this system was somehow linked to the meridian system posited by oriental medicine, upon which acupuncture is based, and the chakra/nadi system of Indian thought and ayuvedic medicine. He began to study these subjects in depth.

Concurrently, Dr Motoyama felt that present-day instrumentation was incapable of measuring the subtler system, which he had come to believe had an electrophysiological manifestation in the body fluid in the connective tissue of the body. He began the study of electrical engineering, which led to his invention of the Apparatus for Measuring the Functioning of the Meridians and their Corresponding Internal Organs (the AMI) in the early 70s, and the Chakra Instrument, a highly sensitive sensor system which monitors subtle fluctuations of the energy field around the human body, and other physiological variables, in 1974.

For the last 15 years, Dr Motoyama has conducted pioneering scientific research with these two devices that has brought him a growing international recognition. A detailed description of his research lies outside the scope of this introduction, but the reader can learn more from other English publications listed in Appendix B. In 1973 the Institute established the International Association for Religion and Parapsychology as a global forum for advancing academic and scientific research into related disciplines. In 1980 the IARP established the Motoyama-Bentov Fund which offers a three month research fellowship to promising students who wish to pursue the holistic study of human existence. Dr Motoyama has published over 50 books and hundreds of articles in Japanese, and lectures frequently.

The bulk of the material for this present book comes from fifty years of what Dr Motoyama calls 'spiritual consultations' that he and the late Reverend Motoyama performed in the Shrine. In a spiritual consultation, a Shrine member comes to Dr Motoyama with a problem. Dr Motoyama meditates with him or her, and looks back psychically over their present and former lives to find the root cause of the problem. He may look into the future to see the probable outcome of the situation if the subject does not alter his or her behaviour. Then he comes back to the present and suggests the most appropriate course of action to remedy the situation.

Through years of spiritual discipline, Dr Motoyama has attained the ability to unify his being with manifestations of the Absolute that he refers to variously as the higher being,

God, expanded consciousness. In this unified state, which transcends the limits of time and space, he is able to directly and clearly perceive the past, the future, and the non-physical dimensions of existence that are connected to the physical realm. In this unified state, his consciousness is able to connect directly with an object in the external world and to affect it. This enables him, for instance, to cure the illness of a person who is in a physically distant location when such action is appropriate.

Over the last fifty years, Dr and Reverend Motoyama have performed more than 40,000 of these consultations. They have drawn two consistent conclusions from their work. The first is that human beings are born onto the earth many times. The second is that the continuum of birth, life, death, and rebirth is governed by the universal principle of karma, the moral law of cause and effect that assumes that every action an individual takes will bear an equivalent result at some point in time.

Dr Motoyama firmly believes that the purpose of existence is the spiritual evolution of the individual. He claims that the essence of this evolutionary process is a universal one, and that there is an Absolute Existence which transcends yet encompasses all the traditional religious and spiritual paths that presently exist and that have existed. Rather than establishing a new ideology, he and his mothers have been interested in working to understand the process of spiritual evolution in a way that can be applied to any individual's specific circumstance.

Dr Motoyama contends that a coherent understanding of karma and reincarnation are crucial to the process of spiritual evolution. Accordingly, as he states in his preface (page 2), this book is 'not an argument for or against the truth of karma and reincarnation'. Instead, it is an attempt to explain how these principles work.

I myself studied and worked closely with Dr Motoyama in Tokyo from 1975 to 1980, and we maintain a warm association. He and his gracious wife, Mrs Kaoru Motoyama, have been unfailing in their patient support of my efforts to translate and edit this often difficult material into English. The manuscript was completed through close cooperation with the International Division of the Institute of Religious Psychology. I would especially like to thank Ms Kiyomi Kuratani of the Translation Department for her painstaking help in translation and continued editorial assistance. I also wish to thank Dr Arthur Thornhill for reviewing the translations and offering invaluable advice.

Rande Brown Ouchi
New York

PREFACE

The primary fact of historical existence is that all things, both living and inanimate, come into being and later vanish.

This holds true on every scale. The galactic system itself has not always existed. It was born about ten billion years ago and at some point in the future it will die. During the time our universe has been in existence it has gradually produced the sun, the earth, and an environment able to support life as we know it. It gave birth to the human race a relatively short time ago, a few million years at most. During the time that billions of individual human beings have lived and died, we have collectively evolved a civilization capable of landing a man on the moon.

What governs this process of birth and death, of growth and development? Present-day scientists tend to rely on the various theories of evolution in search for these answers. I myself am a scientist, with a doctorate in psychophysiology, but feel that a scientific approach to these questions has serious shortcomings.

The main problem is that scientific theories of evolution deal only with the physical dimension, which is but one aspect of a much more complicated reality. When and if they are ever proven, these theories are inherently incapable of explaining anything beyond the facts of physical development. But what of the much larger question of the evolution of the human mind, the human spirit?

Along with being a scientist, I am also a Shinto priest. Through years of strict religious discipline, I have managed to awaken to states of consciousness that enable me to see beyond the limited dictates of time and space. In my role as a spiritual guide and healer, I have looked into the development – past, present, and future – of literally thousands of people who have come to our shrine in Tokyo for help, over the past fifty years. One of the many things I have learned is that, surprisingly, the human mind has not evolved very much over the last ten thousand years. There is less difference than one might expect between modern man and his more primitive antecedents.

My experiences as a priest seem to substantiate more ancient theories of evolution, particularly those so carefully detailed in the yogic tradition of Hinduism. Simply put, this system asserts that the purpose of all existence is an ongoing evolution that ultimately results in attainment of the Absolute (or Unification with God) and that human beings die and are reborn repeatedly until they have reached this goal. The principle that governs this process of reincarnation is the law of cause and effect, or 'karma', as it is generally known.

This book is not an argument for or against the truth of karma and reincarnation. It is, rather, an explanation of these mechanisms from an anecdotal and theoretical standpoint. The information is based on a lifetime of experiences with the past and the future that have guided me to formulate some general principles about karma that I believe are universally applicable.

I feel with increasing intensity that the most important thing for the future of humankind is not the ever increasing rewards of an affluent, materialistic lifestyle, but is, rather, the spiritual evolution of the race. It also appears that one fundamental necessity for accelerated spiritual evolution is a thorough understanding of the realities of our existence. And I don't believe this is possible without understanding the process of reincarnation and the details of karmic law. It is through this understanding that we can begin to learn ways to free ourselves from the bondage of karma, to transcend the limits of the physical dimension, and to evolve into the Enlightened Being that we are all destined to become.

INTRODUCTION

Spiritual Consultation

My spiritual mother, Odaisama, was a profoundly gifted teacher and healer who began my spiritual training when I was five years old. She founded Tamamitsu Shrine, of which I am now the head priest, in 1933. The Shrine is dedicated to a manifestation of Absolute God named Tamamitsu-Okami. This deity manifested to Odaisama in a divine vision giving prophecies about the future of the world, including the occurrence and outcome of the Second World War, and directing her to work for peace. During the revelation she heard the words, 'God has no need of name or rank; Tamamitsu is simply the name I have given you to address me. "Tama" means jewel and "mitsu" means light and their combination represents both divinity, wisdom and compassion.'

Odaisama was directed to institute a service for our parishioners that we call 'spiritual consultations'. Odaisama performed these for many years and I now continue the practice. A spiritual consultation is a direct communication with the appropriate manifestation of Higher Being about a specific problem that a parishioner is experiencing. Through meditation and prayer I unify with the Higher Being, which enables me to see detailed information about the cause of the problem and the ways in which the person can overcome it.

In the vast majority of cases the problem turns out to have its root in a previous incarnation. After thousands of such experiences, I feel I can unequivocally state that we all have had past lives and that our present situations are directly related to these previous incarnations. In fact, actions from past lives are *at the moment* creating who you are right now.

I will give many examples of actual consultations throughout this book, to clarify types of karma and to show how it affects real lives. Let me begin by introducing the following case history of Ms Y. (Although the initials used throughout this text are the first letters of the actual family names, in this case only 'Y.' is used instead of the real initial upon the Y. family's request. At the same time, the actual name of the temple, locations, etc. have been eliminated or initialized in order to protect Y.'s privacy.)

The Case of Ms Y.

Mrs Y. has been a devoted member of the Tamamitsu Shrine for over 35 years. She has an accomplished and prosperous family. Her youngest daughter, however, began to suffer from severe clinical depression the year she turned 21. Her mother brought her to the shrine and asked for a spiritual consultation on the matter.

When I enter samadhi, a unified consciousness that is the highest state of meditation, I am able to see into the past. In Ms Y.'s case, the first thing I saw was a samurai who lived about 350 years ago. As I concentrated upon him, I learned that his name was Hachirouemon Nakanose. He was the chief retainer to a famous warlord, Kiyomasa Kato and lived in the Suwa region, which is located about 150 miles north-west of Tokyo.

This was taking place during the Japanese medieval period when two political factions, the Toyotomi and the Tokugawa, were warring for control of the country. The final battle of this major civil war was at a place called Sekigahara; the Tokugawa emerged victorious and went on to rule Japan for 267 years. I saw that Nakanose had fought in this decisive battle.

I then saw a large stately tomb with Nakanose's name inscribed upon it in K. Buddhist temple.

As for his connection with our suffering Ms Y., I saw that Nakanose had been her father in that incarnation. As his daughter she had fallen passionately in love with a young man who was not considered suitable for her station and whom she was not allowed to marry. Her sorrow was so great that it killed her – she committed suicide in her early twenties.

I also saw that the young girl, along with her mother, had been a devout Buddhist who had worshipped Amida Buddha (Amida Buddha is the main deity of the Pure Land Sect, and it represents the light of everlasting life) in a temple near their home in Suwa.

As for her present-day relationships, I saw that Ms Y. had reincarnated into the same family constellation. Nakanose had been reborn as her maternal uncle, of whom she was exceptionally fond. Her mother in the previous life is her mother again in this one. Her lover was reborn as her older brother.

The cause of her depression was her attachment to her former love and to the resulting sorrow. This attachment, the emotions and thoughts that occurred as a result of the unfulfilled love, remained in her soul after her physical death. When she reincarnated in this life and reached the same age, the sorrowful mind manifested and overtook her.

Her tragedy became the basis for her reincarnation in this body. The attachments to her intense emotions were kept as seeds in her spiritual body between incarnations here on earth. The seeds became the cause of Ms Y.'s reincarnation after her mother in that life had incarnated again as her mother now, and the lover as her brother. The karma of this group, the causal relation among them, had become active and through this connection she was reincarnated. When she reached the same age now as when the incident had occurred in the former life, her strong affection for her lover and her subsequent sorrow rose to the surface and she became ill.

To dispel her depression, Ms Y. needed to detach from the long-held emotion. She had to recognize that its source was deep in the mind belonging to her past life. I counselled her to pray daily to God for help in gaining the necessary detachment, and to investigate the facts of the case as I had seen them to help her come to an intellectual acceptance of reincarnation.

When I first told Ms Y. and her mother what I had seen, they were very surprised because, in truth, their maternal family did come from Suwa. They knew of K. temple because it had been their family temple for generations. Her uncle, in particular, was drawn to the temple and had made pilgrimages to it. They knew I was unaware of any of this information before consultation. However, they had never heard of Hachirouemon Nakanose. I suggested they go to Suwa to look for evidence of his existence.

They soon made the trip, and began their investigation by looking up the name Nakanose in the local telephone book. It wasn't listed. They then made a visit to the resident priest of K. temple, who was well into his eighties at that time. They asked if the grave of someone named Hachirouemon Nakanose was located within the temple precincts. He replied that yes, the tomb of Nakanose had been there until a few years ago. He had been approached by Nakanose's descendents, a family of fishmongers now known as Nakagawa, who had moved from Suwa to another town. They had asked permission to move the tomb as well, which they then did. The priest went on to tell Mrs Y. and her daughter that in a corner of the temple there was still a shrine dedicated to Kiyomasa Kato. This had been built hundreds of years ago as a contribution from Hachirouemon Nakanose. Ms Y. and her mother were delighted that their search had turned up such positive results.

The next summer they went back to Suwa to see if they could find the temple where they had both worshipped Amida Buddha. They found a man knowledgable in local lore who gave them a list of eight possibilities – old temples where Amida might have been enshrined. They brought the list back to me. As I stared at it awhile, I had the realization that S. temple, one of the eight, was the temple they were looking for.

In the summer of the next year, the third since the consultation concerning Nakanose, they returned to Suwa and, with the aid of a detailed map, found S. temple, where they had worshipped Amida Buddha in the past life. It is a very old pagoda located, it turns out, close to K. temple. Amida Buddha was enshrined there. They both felt a profound sense of familiarity and deep spiritual connection to the temple.

On the way back from S. temple they went to the municipal library to check the historical archives of the province. They found the entry 'Nakanose, Hachirouemon' listed in a medieval record. This was followed by a brief description: 'K. Temple, a retainer of Kiyomasa Kato (1562-1611)'. They had found historical proof that Hachirouemon Nakanose had actually existed 350 years ago.

During this three-year period, as Ms Y. devotedly continued her daily prayers and was able to detach from her past situation, her depression gradually lifted. She is now successfully managing her own art gallery in Tokyo.

Karma

The point I wish to illustrate with this example is that Ms Y.'s illness and family situation are directly linked to her past life. She is not a discrete being limited to the present world. Neither are any of us. As many religions have taught throughout the ages, we human beings have an existence that is much deeper and wider than that which is manifest in this dimension. The nucleus of the self, the soul, is like the stitching of a garment in which one side of the cloth represents life and the other, death. In the same way as the thread of the garment runs from one side of the cloth to the other, so the soul continues to exist from one life to the next.

The self is a continuous phenomenon that is ruled by the laws of cause and effect, by karma. Every action causes a reaction. Both positive and negative circumstances are caused by karma, as well as the general characteristics of a personality. Karmic laws, when understood, explain how an innocent child can unexpectedly grow into a very violent adult. Karmic laws help us to understand why a wonderful person does nothing but suffer, or why a person with a rotten character manages to be a success. We expect good actions in this life to produce good results. When they don't, we have to look into the long, many generational process of the individual to find the reason.

Although karma controls every aspect of life, it is important to realize that one is *able to change his or her karma and to affect the way the past manifests in the here and now.* The point of a spiritual consultation, in fact, is to teach the person ways to dissolve the specific karma that is manifesting problematically.

I have grown to believe that the reason we are born here on earth is to work on the dissolution of the various karmas that bind us to this dimension in order to advance to a point where we are able to transcend karma completely.

Each individual is born into a web of interrelated karmic influences. Every one is more or less influenced by at least five categories of karma: personal (individual), familial, local, national and global. I will explain what these are and how they interact. We will also see that the way karma manifests is affected by the way one lives one's life. It is not predetermined that a certain act performed in a past life must necessarily bear, let us say, one hundred karmic fruits in this life. It isn't that simple. Depending on one's present state of consciousness, lifestyle, and degree of faith, a past act can manifest as only one fruit, or a hundred, or a thousand, or none at all.

The instructions given in a spiritual consultation help to ease the severity of karmic manifestation or to dissolve a certain karma completely. These instructions usually outline practices to follow in three areas: behaviour modification, prayer, and meditation.

The instructions and practices given are often difficult, because they deal with dissolving karma directly. And each person must dissolve the karma he or she has created by him or herself: a person is completely responsible for his or her own karma. There are no real shortcuts. A teacher can help a person get from point A to point B, but he can't make the journey in place of the disciple. Teachers can't carry their disciples from start to finish on their backs. They can point out the direction to go, indicate the easiest path, and lend a helping hand when a disciple is exhausted, but the individual must actually make the journey by him or herself.

This journey is one that leads a person to a point where, through detachment and dissolution, one is able to transcend karma at the same time that one is alive in the world of karma. This point is a great step forward towards the state of Enlightenment.

I find the world we live in to be a profoundly miraculous place. I am continually struck by wonder at the fact that everything in the world arises out of nothingness. And I feel that every existence, even an existence that appears bad or evil, needs to be treasured. In the journey of waves across the ocean, we see a continual change between highness and lowness. We don't call the high good and the low bad, but recognize that if the low places did not exist as a base, the high places could not exist either. The summit of a mountain could not exist without the foot. The whole is composed of its parts. When one comes to understand karma for what it is, one realizes the inherent interconnectedness of all beings. While still existing in this world, one can simultaneously experience the existence of higher reality.

Again, I believe that the purpose of life is to dissolve karma, all types of karma. One is not only responsible for his or her personal karma, but for national and global karma as well. We can liken the totality of existence to a river that is running to the world of Enlightenment. The river courses past mountains, races through narrow gorges, and cascades over steep drops. Let us say that each drop of water in the river is an individual human being. The river can only run freely to the extent that each drop is pure. As individuals dissolve and purify their karmas, national and global karma will dissolve naturally as a result. The Absolute has manifested on earth in many saintly forms throughout history to teach us how to do this. I believe, for example, that Lord Tamamitsu is working through our shrine to help the solar system in its movement towards perfection. And there are similar manifestations happening all throughout the world.

Within the vast aggregate, individuals exist. Each human being has an importance and an intrinsic duty to this existence. The total whole of the parts is what moves our world. So if each part is not purified, the whole cannot become pure. When even one small human being dies, the living whole is affected. Every person contains within himself the condensation of divine power and limitless possibilities. When everyone is able to realize this potential, we will reach the final point in time when all will become one with God.

It is my earnest wish that the information contained within the following pages will help you to understand your own karma and how you can more effectively dissolve it.

CHAPTER ONE

Individual Karma:
Life and Death

The Three Dimensions

The karma and reincarnation of any individual existence functions within the structure of a multi-dimensional reality. As people, or human beings, we exist simultaneously in three dimensions of being: the physical, the astral, and the causal. These are the three dimensions of existence that directly comprise the earth. Over the course of time, our bodies and souls incarnate into and out of these planes through a process we call 'being born' and 'dying'.

A spirit manifest (living) on earth as a human being has three bodies: a physical, an astral, and a causal. A spirit manifest (living) in the astral dimension as an astral being has two bodies: an astral and a causal. A spirit manifest as itself in the causal dimension has just one body: a causal one.

While on earth we possess a corresponding mind, or consciousness, to each of the three bodies. The mind/body complexes overlie and interpenetrate one another. The physical is the smallest of the three and the causal is the largest, extending beyond the physical body in a surrounding oval.

Each body-mind has within itself seven energy centres for controlling the vital energy and a system of energy channels. These channels are known in Sanskrit as nadis, and the centres controlling them are known as chakras. The chakras also work as centres of interchange between neighbouring dimensions. On the following page is an illustration of where they are located.

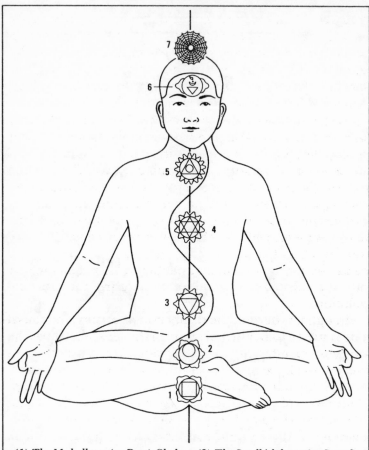

(1) The Muladhara (or Root) Chakra; (2) The Svadhishthana (or Sacral) Chakra; (3) The Manipura (or Solar Plexus) Chakra; (4) The Anahata (or Heart) Chakra; (5) The Vishuddhi (or Throat) Chakra; (6) The Ajna (or Brow) Chakra; (7) The Sahasrara (or Crown) Chakra.

The astral body/mind is the repository of all desire and all emotion, and unconsciously determines much of our behaviour when we exist within normal human limits. Both the physical and astral bodies are characterized by duality, the qualities of attraction and repulsion, positive and negative. The physical body sustains itself through the attraction and intake of air, food – all the elements that nourish and sustain it. When functioning in a healthy manner, the body rejects all substances that are harmful or unnecessary to its maintenance, maintaining a balanced relationship to the external environment. When this balance is broken, sickness and abnormality result. Similarly, the astral body attracts what it desires and rejects what it does not desire.

The causal body is the same as the Christian concept of the spirit (as the astral body is to the notion of soul), in that it is the highest part of our being, the part closest to God. At the moment of creation, the individual is differentiated from the One, and the causal body is born. The causal body is that most closely related to the Absolute; as such, it is beyond duality. Accordingly, it is neither male nor female. All the elements necessary for existence are combined here in perfect equilibrium of pure life energy. The urge to realize this part of our selves and thereby to regain identity with the Absolute engenders the desire for spiritual evolution.

Though it is beyond the distinction of duality, the causal body is still an individuated entity in the sense that it has the power to manifest in diverse forms. The physical is its grossest form, the astral its subtle form. When we are born, we are conscious only in the physical realm. As our consciousness evolves, we gradually become aware of and gain control over the astral realm as well. As we become totally conscious of the ascending dimensions of being, we break through at last into awareness of the causal body. This is the springboard from which total reunification with Absolute, undifferentiated consciousness, can take place.

The three dimensions that we exist in as individuals are part of a much larger reality. Beyond the causal dimension are various dimensions of Divine Being, of God. And each and every dimension is subsumed in the Absolute, whose creative aspect gives rise to all the forms and dimensions of reality as represented in this diagram.

Before discussing in detail how the physical world is related to the other dimensions, let us examine their characteristics in some detail.

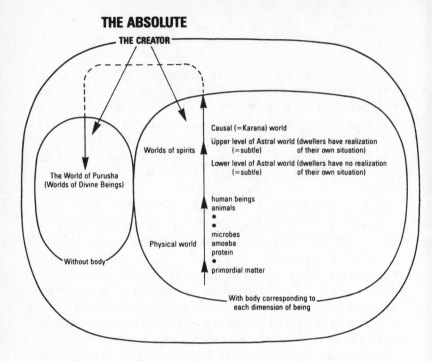

The Astral Dimension: Lower and Higher

The astral dimension is the other side of life; it is where most people exist after they die. The astral dimension has two divisions, the lower and the higher. The lower astral is similar to the popular notions of hell and purgatory. The higher astral corresponds to the general idea of heaven.

The controlling principle of the astral dimension is the mind, just as matter is the controlling principle here on earth. It is a world of ideas. Essentially, this means that in the astral dimension thought creates reality. The mind has a direct effect on the external environment – you get what you want. Astral beings do possess a body, but it is much more elastic than the rigid shells we walk around with here on earth. Otherwise, astral beings are quite similar to who they were when they existed here on earth.

As one's consciousness evolves, one is able to see the astral dimension and to communicate directly with those living in it.

The basic difference between the lower and higher astral is that the lower is inhabited by beings who project a contentious negativity and emotional attachment whereas the higher is peopled by souls who project a more harmonious positivism.

The Lower Astral

The lower astral realm is somewhat like the dream state here on earth. It is similar to a recurring nightmare that is beyond the ability of your conscious mind to stop. In the lower astral dimension, beings are living the nightmare, and they can't wake up – they no longer have the power of the physical plane consciousness, or reason, to separate themselves from the emotions engendered by the dream.

Spirits in the lower astral are trapped in intensely emotional states. The more negative the condition of the astral mind, the more miserable the suffering. The spirits' degree of attachment, whether it be to pain, anger, hatred, despair, physical passion or whatever, holds them prisoner. This attachment can take many long years to wear itself out, and all the while the being's negative thoughts continue to affect his or her existence and the surrounding astral environment.

I know a man named Mr S. whose father died of lung cancer. During my dealings with Mr S. I have had cause to encounter his father who is presently existing in the lower astral dimension. Although he no longer possesses actual lungs, he is suffering terribly from lung pain. He is still directing his mind to the pain he suffered while on earth, and that mind has created actual suffering for him now. He is stuck and can't move into the higher astral dimension. This is a common condition in the lower astral dimension.

The Higher Astral

The higher astral dimension is also similar to the world of dreams here on earth. It is also a world of conception, a realm in which thoughts effect real changes in oneself and in one's surroundings. It is a world where it is possible, if one is content, to remain in the same condition for a very long time.

Here is such an example. Our Shrine and Institute are located on a tract of land bordering a beautiful park in Tokyo. After purchasing the land, I felt the presence of a very old soul exerting a protective influence over the property. Upon closer inspection, I realized that the soul was a powerful tribal leader who had lived on this land 3,500 years ago. He died and has been in the higher astral dimension all this time. We have since erected a small shrine to him to ensure the protection of the land and worship him as Jinushi Okami.

This tribal leader and his people continue to live in the deep past. Their world is thickly wooded. Wild dogs run freely. They live in small villages, make their own pottery, reside in neolithic style structures. The chieftain of this tribe still lives a luxurious life, pampered by his many wives. And all this is going on in the astral dimension at the same time and in the same place that we are living out our modern lives in the physical dimension. I have been able to make some contact with this entity and he has come to have some understanding of the way in which the world has changed, but he is happy with his ancient ways and does not wish to change anything.

He is just one example of someone who is satisfied to be existing in a dimension where thoughts create reality. People in similarly contented situations may choose to stay that way for hundreds, even thousands, of years. After all, in such dimensions people don't have to suffer from any physical desires – it is clearly a less troublesome state of existence. But, in parallel to the lower astral spirit who is trapped in negative emotion and can not move, people who get too comfortable in the higher astral dimension make no evolutionary progress at all. They are so completely and subjectively consumed by their own conceptions that they are also stuck, running on the spot. They are not moving any closer to Enlightenment.

However, the vast majority of people do come back to this earth as soon as they have the chance. This does not mean they necessarily feel that this world is better than where they were, but it is evidence of their great attachment to physical reality. It is very rare to find someone who really believes, 'I've had more than enough and I'm never coming back.' And even if they say it, they usually end up coming back anyway. Most people are born again within one hundred years of their last death.

Birth

The process of being born a human being is actually quite complicated and controlled by many regulations. It is more difficult to be born here from the lower astral realms than it is from the higher, for instance.

In the lower astral realms of the spiritual world there are a multitude of beings who want to be born onto this earth. However, it is not possible for all of them to achieve this. There is a specific screening process, a set of conditions which must be met before a being is allowed to re-enter our world. Although maintained and controlled by karma, the screening process itself is a Divine device to protect us here on earth from the more negative elements of existence. The lower astral beings who are rejected by the screening process are left with no choice but to continue their growth in the lower realm, no matter how slowly, inching their way closer to true Awakening.

One type of lower astral spirit I encounter frequently is what I call 'foetal spirits' – beings who have been miscarried or aborted into the lower astral realm. Foetal spirits are quite bizarre looking – they are wrinkled all over, have large goggling eyes, and emit a strange glow. Many people who have aborted a child carry with them a deep sense of guilt. In certain cases, however, this sense of guilt is not justified. I have come to this conclusion by closely examining foetal spirits themselves. The individuals who have the karma to become foetal spirits tend to be extraordinarily selfish. They tend to be the type of people who would do anything to promote their own self-interest, even killing to get what they want. In effect, our world is better off if these people are not born into it. I want to be clear that this does not mean that I am necessarily pro-abortion, which I am not, but wish to indicate that the Absolute in its infinite wisdom has laid down intricate guidelines to protect us from the worst elements of existence and that sometimes abortion is used for this purpose.

The guidelines that regulate the process of being born on the earth are more far-reaching than those that regulate individual karma. They are the principles that regulate and maintain the delicate balance between the physical and astral realms, and are karmic principles of both restriction and harmony. Basically these principles act as a limitation on who can be born here. The fact that you are alive proves that you have met the basic requirements.

Again, most of the individuals who are not allowed to leave the lower astral realms are extremely negative. This negativity is caused by undue and extreme self-attachment, what we call 'evil' here on earth. Following the principle that thought produces reality, these lower astral beings create a state of being which, as a conglomerate, fits the common notion of hell. Naturally, beings who exist in these places want to get out of them as quickly as possible: they see being born on earth as their escape. Using the power of this overwhelming desire, a being can sometimes force its way through the safety net and get itself conceived, but such conception rarely results in birth. Usually the beings are miscarried or are aborted, and are sent back to the lower astral realm where they came from. They may repeat this process a number of times. Occasionally, the desire to be born may be so tremendous that the being manages to slip through the restrictive screening and attain birth. These beings may be born deformed, as a result of the unnaturalness of their method of entry.

Fortunately, most children are born from the astral into the physical plane as healthy little people. And they come with a full karmic package.

Many parents wonder at the fact that their children, though physically similar, have such startlingly different personalities. In Japanese we have the proverb, 'Frogs breed frogs.' In English you say, 'Like father, like son.' We also have the proverb, 'Eagles bear falcons.' Or in English, 'Black hens lay white eggs.' These seemingly conflicting proverbs all appear true.

I do a lot of work with computers. It fascinates me how one small change in a program can cause it to produce a completely different result. Heredity likewise depends on a program, the linkage of a certain number of genes. If one of the genes is damaged, or if the order of the line-up is changed, the child produced inherits the changes. There are many ways for such changes to occur, and, even if the major pattern is the same, one small change can produce tremendous differences between two individuals. Although this is a sound medical explanation of how one set of parents gives birth to such different children, it in no way explains how these minute changes in gene linkage come about. I believe they come about in response to the karmic make-up of the individual.

If one can see differences in the children of the same parents, the variety widens as one looks in on, say, an elementary school class. Each child's own quirks and talents are very obvious at this stage. The children have not yet accumulated much knowledge about this world and exist more as raw material. Many of the characteristics a child possesses represent a continuation of his or her unique nature from a previous incarnation.

For a few years after birth, a child has memories of the astral dimension he or she has so recently left. The quality of those memories is similar to that which an adult may experience when you wake up from a dream and are steeped in the feeling of the experience but can't quite remember the details. The astral memory a child possesses is one reason for children's frankness and naivety. Children have just come from a place where desire and visualization create reality. It can be very difficult for children to accept the fact that they can no longer wish things or situations into being. They have to learn that in this world they are shackled with a physical body and that this restricts their exercise of total selfishness and wilfulness. Some children become very dark and depressed when they are forced to realize that they are locked up inside their own tight little shell.

Lately in the home-life sections of the Japanese newspapers there has been a rash of stories about children with severe phobias and other psychological conditions like autism. These problems obviously cause suffering not only in the child but also for the whole family. Following is the story of such a child.

A mother and father from Kamakura came to see me. Their son was suffering terribly from school phobia, among many other fears and behavioural problems. The parents were not able to understand the source or cause of their son's suffering and were extremely worried. The family itself is an old and wealthy one, and the son is the only male child in a family of girls. The parents admitted to spoiling their children, but didn't feel that was enough to cause the extent of the boy's problems.

I performed a spiritual consultation about the cause of these problems, and found out that the boy had been a commander in the powerful Heike clan in a former life. This was in the 12th century, when the Heike clan was under attack from the Genji clan. The Genji had a powerful leader named Yoritomo, who wound up establishing his shogunate in Kamakura and founding the Kamakura period (1185-1333).

The boy had been the overseer of the entire Kanto area for the Heike and, as such, was a very important person.

Yoritomo wanted the Kanto area and tried to take it by force. At one point the Heike defeated Yoritomo at a place called Ishibashiyama, but eventually Yoritomo recouped his strength and went on to conquer the entire area. Several hundred of the Heike warriors tried to flee Kamakura by ship to a town on the Izu Peninsula called Usami. When they got there, however, Yoritomo's forces were ready and waiting. They captured all the Heike warriors and slew them one by one on the beach.

The boy in our story was one of those who was killed. When I spoke to his mother later, I asked her if her son had ever exhibited any negativity towards the Usami area. Shocked, she replied that, yes, this had been another source of conflict. Apparently the family owns a summer house in the very town of Usami, and though the other children love to go there, the son was intractable in his refusal to go near the place. This had totally baffled his parents. She also told me that they are direct descendants of the Heike family, a fact I was not aware of when I began the enquiry. (In fact, I rarely know many specifics about a person when he or she comes for a spiritual consultation for the first time. Most people are at first quite sceptical of the process and need to test me a bit, so they rarely offer much information. This is fine, as such prior knowledge is irrelevant to the efficacy of the consultation. If, however, someone is mentally defying me to a strong degree, I psychically see a thick cloud surrounding them. In such cases I will tell the person that I don't feel they are serious enough about the consultation and that we shouldn't attempt to do it at the present time. If a person doesn't come to me openly and honestly, I cannot connect with their being effectively.)

We can see why this child was suffering so miserably. He died in a state of complete terror, after watching hundreds of his compatriots lined up on the beach and decapitated. Locked in his emotions are both the intense attachment to the life he had at that time and the unspeakable horror of his death. When a being moves into the astral dimension holding onto such attachment and terror, the soul continues experiencing much suffering there potentially for a long time to come. In this way, the boy was still suffering, and was manifesting his suffering in part as a strong aversion to Usami, the site of his summer home, and phobias and behavioural problems in his hometown of Kamakura. Usami is where he lost his life, and Kamakura was the victorious capital of his former enemies.

Death

The feelings, emotions, and thoughts which make up the unconscious (manas in Sanskrit) are the minds we take with us to the astral dimension when we die. The feelings and emotions one experiences at death are key factors in determining the kind of existence one will lead in the other world. It is important to try to stand firm in death, to watch with detachment as the old identity is cast off. If one dies in a great state of attachment one is likely to end up in a lower astral realm. People who die in a state of abject terror often find themselves in this situation. Moreover, the mind-set at death can reappear in an amplified form at the time of rebirth into this world, as I found in the case of the unaccountably miserable child.

Death does not necessarily entail suffering, however.

My natural mother, Seiko-sensei, and I were lying asleep on either side of Odaisama the night she died. Odaisama did not reveal herself to me in my dreams that night, but I cherish the first clear vision I had of her after her death.

It took place after the funeral, following the cremation. Odaisama appeared to me wearing the 12 layered kimono I had last seen her in and, with divine countenance, said, 'My body has been committed to ashes but my being has not. I am now with God.'

For about a month after the vision, Odaisama appeared to me in a reclining position and it seemed as though she were resting.

From then until now, she often appears as she looked in her twenties and thirties, and is as energetic as she was in that active period of her life when she was travelling throughout Japan doing spiritual practice. Since her death she seems to have attained an even greater understanding of this world, and I often hear her voice at my heart or on the top of my head when I am doing a spiritual consultation about a particularly difficult problem.

It is wonderful when someone can move into a divine realm as quickly as Odaisama was able to. For the majority of human beings, however, death is not quite as easy.

Members of our Shrine often come to request help when one of their family is dying. I go into meditation in front of the altar and usually receive a clear vision of the failing person. If the situation has passed into the critical stage, if the person's pulse has stopped or if the fever is extremely high, the soul usually appears to be floating above the body. Occasionally, with a tremendous concentration of energy, I am able to help the being return to the body.

In the majority of cases, however, the person has reached the end of his or her karmically determined life span and does die. If the person has not reached the end of his or her lifetime, no matter how sick he or she appears, he or she will definitely recover and live until the appointed time of death. When someone dies, what I and the surviving loved ones can do is to help the soul make its passage into the higher astral realms as easily as possible.

Just as most spirits are unaware in life, they are unaware of what is going on in the death process. I will go into the mechanism of dying later on, but for now suffice it to say that most people are not immediately aware that they are 'dead', even after their soul has left their body. The spirit continues to contain and feed on a certain amount of energy it carries over from the physical dimension, and it continues to direct itself towards this plane. This energy dissipates in a week or two and then a difficult period sets in.

The spirit often beings to suffer from unbearable hunger and thirst, a feeling of starvation. This is because it still thinks it is alive yet is unable to find any substance. The spirit may find itself alone in a kind of deep dark pit and cannot figure out where it is or what it is doing there. I have seen this painful condition continue for two or three weeks in some cases, one to two months in others. The individual spirit eventually comes to realize what has happened and to accept the fact of his or her death. Then he or she is ready to move on to the next karmically determined place of existence.

During the difficult period before the soul becomes aware of its new situation, it is a tremendous help if relatives and friends are praying and making offerings on the deceased's behalf. Mourning rituals have a real purpose more primary than that of comforting those left behind. They greatly aid the deceased individual in waking up to the new reality of his or her condition. For this reason, I always feel sorry for people who die with no one around to mourn them because it seems especially difficult for these people to rise up to the higher dimensions. People who are killed in battle or in an unexpected accident have a particularly difficult time of it because they tend to be paralyzed by the terror that overcame them at the moment of death and are not able to move out of the terror into another state. It is especially difficult for these beings to realize that they are dead. Intercessionary prayers, particularly those of spiritually evolved people, can be a great help in facilitating any suffering spirit's passage to the next stage.

On Being Human

Through my work I have come to believe that existence as a human being on the physical plane is an extraordinary opportunity that should be deeply cherished. The Absolute has created this world, within Its universal government, as a specific arena where the evolution of consciousness can take place. Beings who make the most of this opportunity and reach a highly evolved state can move into the embodied causal plane or beyond into the divine realms of pure consciousness after death; they are free to make rapid spiritual progress on those planes and to interact at will with the lower planes. A causal being appears disembodied to an astral being – the astral individual perceives the causal one as a dazzling sphere of light or as a shining halo. Causal beings often act as guardian angels to individuals with whom they have karmic relationships or as protectors of certain areas or communities. However, it is almost impossible for the spirits in the astral world to pass directly into the causal dimension. To accomplish the move they must attain a state of self-awareness and freedom from attachment to their thoughts and emotions that is difficult to accomplish in the astral dimension because of the inherent structure of that dimension itself. Since it is a dimension ruled by emotion and thought, there is little leverage to separate oneself from obsessive attachment to emotion and thought. The astral is a subjective rather than objective reality, one in which mind and matter are more intimately connected than they are here on earth and where it is very difficult for consciousness to undergo significant evolution.

Herein lies the genius of the physical plane. We are necessarily born with physical bodies, and physical reality is the lever that enables us to separate from our mental processes. To give a simple example, suppose you are staring out of the window obsessed with a lover who has rejected you or a promotion that you failed to get. No matter how lost in thought you may be, eventually you are going to get hungry. As the hunger grows more insistent it temporarily causes you to disengage from your obsession and concentrate on the physical actions necessary to fulfil this desire. In a similar fashion, we are able to use our will and our reason to separate us from negative attachment patterns and bad habits and, ultimately, to dissolve the karma that binds us here.

Compared with the matter of the astral world, physical matter, though connected, holds a greater degree of independence from the mind. If you concentrate on a spoon lying on the table in front of you and mentally command it to move, chances are it won't. The mental desire to overcome an illness will not produce an instant cure. When we wish to control matter in the physical world we must first make mental cognition of it through the senses, and then act upon it in a physical way, using the body or a physical instrument. Because the power of the physical is so much stronger here than in the astral dimension, there are more chances to free ourselves from attachments through the agency of our senses and physical and mental activity. It is easier for a mind to attain self-reflection and spiritual growth in the physical world than in the astral world. In other words, God made this world for us to make our spiritual growth easier than it is in the astral world.

If you are reading this, not only do you have the great fortune to be born on the physical plane, but thanks to your parents, you have been born as a human being rather than as some other member of the animal or vegetable kingdom.

Monkeys may be perfectly content to be monkeys, but they don't possess the mental capabilities to gain true self-awareness. Learning experiments conducted in the United States on chimpanzees have demonstrated that the animals do have rudimentary thought process. They can be taught to push a certain combination of buttons to ask for juice or to request that someone they don't like be removed from the room. This is useful in that it proves the ability to verbalize and to think are not necessarily connected, but it doesn't prove that monkeys are able to control their emotional reactions.

Human children exhibit a similar level of mental and emotional reaction to the monkey. The main difference between children and adults, in fact, is that adults are more able to control their reactions and the expression of them. If an adult meets someone he doesn't like, he should have the ability to repress a rude negative reaction and to reflect upon his feelings. Unfortunately for society, there are adults whose inability to reflect upon or control their emotions renders them more animal than human.

Pity the poor cow. Before the advent of the machine, cows were yoked and made to plough the fields for hours on end. Soil can be excruciatingly heavy – from morning till night, dragging the plough through acres and acres of earth. And the final reward for all this labour was to end up as beef on somebody's table. Compared to such a life, the lot of a human being is quite special.

CHAPTER TWO

Karma:
A Definition

The Dependent Nature of Self

Karma is basically a result of the spiritual ignorance of the self that mistakenly believes it is an independent entity. As long as the self functions in this state of ignorance it is imprisoned in a continuous process of death and reincarnation within the dimensions of reality that are governed by the law of cause and effect.

Even on a physical level, the notion that we are independent entities is untenable. We don't compose the matter of our bodies ourselves, we require the physical agency of our parents to make us. We can't exist without air, water, or food. As infants we depend on the nurturance of other people's love and affection. Our ability to live as members of human society depends on our awareness of and discipline in social morals. From a genetic, physical, and intellectual standpoint it is clear that a person cannot exist by him or herself but can only live by depending on other forces.

From a spiritual and non-physical standpoint, the existence of every creature in this world is totally dependent on the working of God. This is what Christianity refers to as the working of the Holy Spirit. The existence of the physical world itself is sustained through its mutual dependence on the various spiritual realms. And as human beings, whether conscious of it or not, we live in constant dependent connection to the astral and causal dimensions.

The physical mind and the physical body are mutually dependent – we can only function as complete beings on the basis of this fact. The minds and bodies of the astral and causal dimensions are likewise dependent, but the minds have differing degrees of control over the respective matter of their corresponding dimension.

Buddhism teaches that the nature of reality is 'Sunya' or Empty. This emptiness refers to the fact that nothing has an independent being, all is related. The subject/object distinction does not exist. It is impossible for anything, including the self, to exist by itself.

The ignorant self blindly performs the various actions necessary to maintain and perpetuate its existence. On the physical level the self needs at least to obtain food, shelter, and clothing. The self desires to be as successful at this as possible, which translates into a common desire for materialistic status within society, whatever economic form that society takes.

Intellectually, the self desires to pursue its own interests as well. According to the individual character, the self will enter a field such as music, philosophy, science, technology, politics or whatever to satisfy and develop its mind.

People with any level of education or who are active within a profession all work in society seeking physical and intellectual satisfaction in order to maintain their selves. An early teaching of Buddhism is that all activity can be categorized into three groups: actions of the body, actions of the mouth, and actions of the mind. If a man, for example, wants to become a musician because he loves music he requires the three types of action to accomplish his goal. His will to become a musician is an action of the mind. He communicates his desire to others in order to find a teacher. This is an action of the mouth. Then he must practise on his chosen musical instrument by using parts of his physical body. This is an action of the body.

Let us suppose that as a result of these three actions, the man succeeds in becoming a good musician, pleases many audiences, establishes himself in society, and gains financial security. His self will have attained the physical satisfaction of food, clothing, and shelter, as well as the mental satisfaction of fulfilling its interest. In his case everything seems to have gone well. But this is not always the case in life. Each individual grows in an overall network of various elements such as innate talent, family circumstances, social connections, social environment, current world conditions, changes in natural phenomena and so on, and their reciprocal interactions. These can just as often produce unfortunate results. Our hypothetical musician might have had to give up his musical education half-way for financial reasons, even if he were exceptionally talented. He could have been forced to leave his studies because war broke out or his country's economy was crippled by a major natural disaster. In such an event his profession might be considered superfluous. If he were unable to perform as a musician, he might suffer great frustration that would turn into a strong attachment to music. This attachment could become deeply rooted karma that would manifest sometime in the future.

Attachment to Desire

The human mind has the tendency to form intense attachments. These attachments are the root cause of karma. We supposedly appeared on earth 2 to 5 million years ago. Ever since then, the species has sexually reproduced and eaten food to preserve itself, just like the more primitive animals, though we have had more success in adapting to the environment and have made conspicuous progress. But because we still depend upon these two physical methods for self-preservation, the human instinct to fulfil them is very powerful. It is very difficult for human beings to control sexual desire. Scandals concerning love affairs never cease to exist in this world. Appetite is another instinctive desire that is difficult to control. Without food, physical functioning cannot be maintained. Feuerbach, the materialist, said: 'Man is what he eats.' And he is correct as far as the physical body is concerned. Humans eat everything: beef, chicken, snails, snakes and lizards, as well as wheat, rice and vegetables. We don't hesitate to kill animals for food. We seek to satisfy ourselves without limit. We become desperate when threatened with starvation – something made very clear to my generation of Japanese in the aftermath of World War II. Attachment to instinctive desire is a potent karma producer.

Attachment to Emotion

Attachment to emotion and thought make up the rest of the bulk of karma that defines an individual.

We can define 'emotion', in general, as the condition of the internal mind. This condition is created by the mind's reaction to diverse stimuli. Emotions are of two types, the transient and the sustained.

The simplest emotions are sensory emotions which are triggered by sensory stimuli such as sound and smell. They are often passionate and at the same time transitory feelings. If your life is suddenly threatened, for example, you feel a mixture of fear, shock, and anger. When the danger passes you feel great relief and very happy. Passing mood is another example of the transient type of emotion. If it's a beautiful day and you are healthy and unstressed and taking a walk outside, chances are you will feel high and happy.

The second type of emotion is a more sustained feeling that affects the whole being and is often produced in response to lasting cultural phenomena such as learning, art, or morality.

Both these types of emotions are related in that they are varying stages of the internal landscape as it changes in reaction to the diverse stimuli of the outer world. How is it that these emotions cause karma?

When we behold a magnificent work of art or hear a glorious piece of music, when we step over the threshold of a majestic cathedral, we may feel a profound sense of awe and happiness. This type of aesthetic sentiment does not in and of itself breed karma. Nor does the experience of the transient, passionate emotions.

Emotions occur in reaction to general emotional stimuli: you feel enraptured when listening to beautiful music, you turn away from a foul smell. When someone fondles you, you either feel good or your skin crawls depending on who is doing the fondling. All emotion can be divided into two categories, those that are pleasurable and those that are not. As is the nature of living things, a human being is normally disposed to seek pleasure and to avoid pain. And we react to the same stimulus differently according to time and place. A breath of fragrant perfume is refreshing when you are travelling on an underground train jammed full of sweaty people on a summer afternoon, but the same strong perfume is offensive when it interferes while you are eating something with a subtle aroma. Such reactive, temporary emotions do not in and of themselves create karma.

Karma begins when the emotional pleasure or displeasure produced by a reaction to a stimulus comes to be subjectively differentiated. The emotion produced within individual people to the same stimulus is different. A certain piece of music does not create the same mood in everyone. The smell of incense is relaxing to some, repellent to others (in Japan, because of its association with the Buddhist rituals of death). We come to develop enduring emotional patterns of pleasure or displeasure regarding specific objects, fixed emotional expressions of our likes and dislikes. If an object has been fixed in a pleasurable mode, we seek that object. When we encounter it we are happy, when we cannot get it we are unhappy.

The fixation of these emotional patterns produces differences between individuals and is a key factor in determining a person's character and disposition. The important fact to us here is that *this fixation*, whether for the good or for the bad, *is what causes karma.*

Karmically, the most problematic of the emotions are usually those of the intense, passionate type, such as fear, hatred, and joy. If you are suddenly frightened by something you see, the fear should extinguish when the object frightening you is no longer present. If emotions such as terror, joy, or passion are temporary, they will evaporate when over and leave nothing behind. But if you cling to these emotions, they will accumulate and settle into the deep recesses of your mind, from where they will continue to exert influence on your self. If they are embedded firmly enough, they will carry over from one lifetime into another. As with the phobic boy, stored emotions from the past have the power to affect the present.

In my work with mentally ill patients, I have observed that people suffering from schizophrenia are sometimes people who were involved in murders or other violent deaths in their former lives, the terror of which is the root cause of their present condition. Similarly, it appears to me that many manic-depressives have a tremendous amount of either hate-or-love-attachment stored in them from some previous situation. In a lot of these cases I see lust tightly entwined with these emotions. This seems to be particularly true of depressives, many of whom seem to me to have been hopelessly entangled in love/hate, male/female relationships in former lives, and who to this day are preoccupied with thoughts of sex.

The passionate emotions are able to create deep karma because they possess the power to block out reason.

In Japan, it is said that someone who likes to drink has a 'sake-worm' (sake: rice wine) living in his stomach. My uncle must have been raising ten of them. He drank away his home, he drank away his fields, and still he wasn't satisfied. Karmically, this is a very bad situation. The passionate addiction to alcohol, to the state of temporary well-being it brings, to the insatiable craving itself, throws consciousness into a state of confusion and deeply affects the personality and character of the individual. It is very difficult to dissolve the karma which results from such unreasoned passion.

Attachment to the sustained type of emotion can also be the foundation for karma. Such emotion becomes trouble-some when it is directed towards the 'self' and is allowed to become very strong. Powerful karma-producers here are egotism, pride, vanity, and ambition.

Karmic troubles are often caused by a combination of both types of emotional attachment.

I know one man who was an abbot of the Tendai Sect of Buddhism in his former life. At the present time he is involved in a business which is not directly related to the religious sphere yet one that often brings him into contact with the headquarters of Tendai Buddhism on Mt. Hiei in Kyoto. Whenever he is involved in a large business project there, he can only get about 80% of the job done before something gets in the way of completing the work. This leaves him frustrated and confused. The gentleman himself knows nothing of his former identity, but I am aware that during his former life on Mt. Hiei he had undertaken the construction of a major temple and had died on the verge of its completion.

As the abbot, this man was passionately devoted to the building of the temple, so much so that his regret over his failure was indelibly printed somewhere in his consciousness. In this life he is again faced with the problem of not being able to satisfactorily complete any project concerning the temple complex. In his former life his passions burned and his frustration was great, and residues of these processes continue to create obstacles for him today.

Karma results from mental attachment to an emotion, no matter how ideal. Attachment to a sustained love of knowledge, truth, or wisdom, for instance, produces long-lasting karma.

A person may have undergone years of devoted spiritual discipline and attained a certain level of wisdom and Enlightenment. He teaches others according to the realization he has attained. Then missionaries arrive in his country and begin preaching a religion that derives from a totally different cultural background. The native teacher has not yet attained ultimate Enlightenment, his consciousness is simply more evolved than that of the others around him, and he picks up contradictions between his version of the truth and what the missionaries are teaching. The ensuing religious dispute causes him to attach to his level of wisdom and to get stuck at that point in his evolution. In the same way, religions themselves have been warring with each other since ancient times. Their adherents are more attached to their own self-righteousness than to the ongoing process of self-realization.

Scientists and scholars can fall into the same trap. Having once established a theory, they may cling to it with emotional insistence even when contradictory evidence is discovered. Though supposedly committed to the truth, they are more interested in protecting their emotional investments.

One man I know was a scholar in a former life during the Edo period (1600-1867). He was passionately absorbed in his work, but unfortunately died of pulmonary disease in the midst of his research. In this lifetime he is again an ardent scholar and has suffered from pulmonary disease. But there is a difference between then and now. He is now aware of the conditions of his former life and death and has vowed to dissolve the subsequent karma. Although he is still a devoted scholar, he has transformed his passion into a deep faith in God. Through this process, his frustrations have disappeared, he has cut his karmic ties to lung disease, and his present life is running smoothly.

Attachment to Thought

Attachment to instinctive desire and emotion are two primary factors in the creation of karma. Attachment to thought is a third.

The phenomenon of ideation has both a positive and a negative aspect. The positive aspect manifests as the faculty of creative thought and imagination, the negative one as ideal fantasy which in its extreme form manifests as out and out delusion.

The main difference between ideation and emotion, though both are activities of the mind, is that whereas the emotions are simply conditions of the internal mind, ideation and imagination are two modalities of cerebration that are linked to the outside world.

Both the imagination and fantasy are initially grounded in external reality. Let us examine the mental mechanism involved.

Let us say you take a trip somewhere that you thoroughly enjoy. This experience, experience A if you will, is the sum aggregate of a number of factors – the scenery, the climate, the people you meet, the food you eat. These factors we can label a1, a2, a3 . . . The mind analyses the experience into factors A1, A2, and A3 . . . and reconstructs the experience one more time within itself. The activity of dismantling and reconstructing these various factors for future experience is what we call imagination. If this reconstruction takes place in relation to reality and with a purpose that refers to the outside world, the process is one of productive, creative imagination. When one performs the reconstruction without purpose and without reference to reality, the process is one of idle fantasizing.

Whether ideation takes the form of productive imagination or of fantasy, it is still basically a subjective process. We gradually ascertain whether or not the contents of the imagination are actually useful by acting them out in the real world. Science, through the act of experimentation, confirms whether something it has conceived or imagined holds true in the objective world. Similarly, in everyday life we constantly confirm the validity of what we have imagined through our actions in the outside world. Getting lost, for example, indicate that one's internally imagined map and the form of the objective world are at odds with each other. Normally our lives consist of a series of similar repeated actions, so we don't make that many mistakes. But when confronted with a novel experience about which we have insufficient information, the discrepancy between our internal landscape and the outside world becomes evident.

This discrepancy is most evident in people who live in relative isolation from the real world, notably in psychotics, infants, and the aged.

Psychotic patients are characterized by their inability to discriminate between objective reality and the ideas and images which their powers of imagination have constructed in their own minds. They are in an abnormal, deluded state in which objective and subjective realities are mixed.

It is interesting to note here that geniuses sometimes seem to be as abnormal as psychotics. But there is a major difference between the two. Geniuses gain knowledge of the outside world not only through the simple sensory mechanisms that ordinary people rely on, but are also privy to a system of transcendent intellect and perception which enables them to create images of objects using a freer, wider, and deeper imagination than is normally employed. The knowledge a genius thus obtains is so deeply tied into the real world that it is able to effect truly revolutionary change. The imaginings of psychotics, on the other hand, are not rooted in this deeper intellect nor connected to reality, and they cannot effect such changes in the real world.

Infants are fundamentally different from deluded adults in that their mental deficiencies are simply due to the fact that they have not yet had enough experience of the world in this life and that their faculty of cognition is not yet fully developed. Children are able to receive a lot of information but are not able to grasp the objective meaning of that information. The other day my youngest son pointed at a desk and declared that the desk was really a certain super-hero from a popular cartoon show. This not only shows that he watches too much television, but also that he can take an image received from television and project it onto an object in the real world. The child's mind holds an undifferenti-ated mixture of elements from both the real and imaginary worlds.

As people grow old, their hearing beings to fade, their eyesight grows dim, and they start to interact less and less with the outside world. They sometimes retreat into a private world of their own. One old woman I know complained to me during her husband's wake that he should be there attending to their many guests rather than wandering about by himself someplace. The old man was still very much alive in the imaginary world of the old woman.

A healthy mind is capable of making objective judgements by comparing the ideas produced by the imagination to the reality of the external world by connecting the two to each other. But if someone forgets that the world of ideas is only a product of the subjective imagination and confuses it with external, objective reality, treating the two as though they were equal, serious karmic captivity develops. They begin to live off their imagination as though they were eating their own dreams. Once trapped in the imagination it is difficult to get free.

There are many objects that can hold the mind captive – money, sex, and power are particularly popular here on earth. However, it is important to understand that the object is irrelevant to the fact of the captive state itself. Becoming a slave to one's attachment is extremely restrictive. When consciousness is free and relaxed it can sprout wings and grow large enough to span the heavens. But when it is held captive, it sinks into a deep dark well where it has absolutely no room to move. It becomes difficult to conceptualize taking even one step away to distance oneself from the situation.

All things in the world are ceaselessly changing. And so it is with the human mind. An object which is now A will next become B, or maybe C, or maybe cease to exist altogether. But when the human mind is held captive in one state it remains A, A, A; it defies the natural law of change. Imagine a boat flowing along on the current of a river. A man takes a pole and shoves it into the riverbed, trying to halt the action of the boat. What happens? Since it is unreasonable to try to keep the boat still in the midst of the flow, the boat begins to turn in circles around the centre-point of the pole. Ripples extend outward from the spinning boat to become hindrances to other passing craft. If the state of captivity is very deep, that is, if the pole is entrenched with great force, a whirlpool can ensue. In like fashion, a whirlpool can be created in the human mind, a whirlpool which swallows the essentially dispassionate faculty of reason.

Karma is not created by emotions and ideas themselves, but *by our attachment to them.* The 'self', or ego, is what allows us to live. Yet this same 'self' erroneously thinks it is a discrete entity that exists in opposition to the rest of existence. The mind works to preserve this 'self' by encasing it in a thick karmic shell that it builds through the process of attachment.

Our consciousness is held captive within the restrictive shell or the 'self'. How do we become free? One way is to dissolve karma through learning detachment. The term for this philosophical approach is 'non-action within action'. We will discuss this in greater detail later, but, in brief, this means: acting out the unfolding of one's day to day life continuously but without attachment to the results of the actions, 'just doing'. It is the consciously working to transcend the 'self' while being the 'self', through constantly detaching from the smaller self that is bound by desire. It is a very effective way to transcend the world of karma and make spiritual progress.

CHAPTER THREE

The Varieties of Karma: Marital and Family Karma

It is impossible for an individual to manifest on this earth by him or herself. A person is born through parents into a web of immediate social relationships. There are many a priori connections necessary to be born in a given place at a given time, in fact to be born at all. At the very least, karmic connections must exist to:

> the galaxy
> the earth
> the country
> the locale
> the race/religion
> the family line
> the parents

Viewed against this background of complex and interrelated necessities, individual existence seems like a profound miracle.

But birth happens all the time, and we unfortunately tend to take it for granted. It seems to me that many of our present-day problems are caused by the fact that people do not recognize and respect the great causes that enable them to exist and function on this earth. In this chapter we will explore various examples of suffering caused by disrespect to causal factors such as the earth and our ancestors.

Myriad strands of interrelated karma are involved in the sprouting of 'individual' karmic entities. Individuals appear separate and distinct, but they are not. We are bound together by uncountable, invisible ties. Physically our bodies may seem independent but an infant would die without the care of an adult. Emotionally and psychologically we are interconnected in ways that science is just beginning to fathom.

Before we even begin to explore these connections, let us look at why the phenomenon of connection itself is possible.

Basically, human beings have the ability to bond with each other because we are all grounded in the Absolute, because the source and foundation of our being is identical. Every single aspect of existence is a manifestation of the Absolute, of God. The experiential realization of this brings reunification with the Absolute, the total extinguishing of the individual. We call this Enlightenment.

Any relationship that is possible is precisely so because everything is connected in the Absolute. This is true whether the relationship is between parent and child, husband and wife, brother and sister, master and dog, or a boy and a rock. Ultimate connection already exists. In our individual existences we discover, create, and dissolve relationships as we learn about the nature of existence and evolve towards a state of transcendence. Without karma we would not exist – it is a necessary burden and dissolving it a great teacher.

Karmic bonding between individuals, or human relationship, is possible in the physical, astral, and causal dimensions. Depending on the degree of bonding that occurs in each or any of these dimensions, relationships vary in depth and intensity. This variation is particularly evident in sexual/marital bonding, one of the strongest bonds that there is here on earth.

Marital Karma: Varieties of Bonding

The sexual bonding of two individuals who commit to each other as a couple, usually in the form of marriage, is the prerequisite to birth and therefore the foundation of family karma. Generally, it can occur in five different ways:

1. Two beings are linked together by the knots of their previous karmic relationship, whether these knots be caused by attachment to their mutual happiness or to their mutual suffering.
2. Two beings unite in the higher level of their individual spirits, in the causal dimension, a level which always remains in an immaculate condition.
3. A unified entity in a relatively high (divine) spiritual dimension splits in two, manifests as a man and a woman on this earth, and the two marry.
4. Two beings are temporarily bound together by materialistic, physical passion.
5. Two beings of deep religious faith are united through the intercession of a Higher Power.

The fundamental principle of 'self-attachment' has two basic aspects. The first of these is that the 'self' begins to believe that it is all that exists of its being. The second aspect is that the 'self' believes it is unique and creates the distinction that 'others' are different from 'self'. This is the state of consciousness that most ordinary human beings function within, and is the level upon which the most common type of marital bonding occurs.

As soon as individuals begin to function from the position of 'self', karma is produced. Good and evil, happiness and unhappiness, and a myriad of other distinctions are born. Each of these distinctions is created by the 'self', a 'self' that stumbles blindly onwards, completely unaware of the increasing amount of karma that it is accumulating. The 'self' mistakenly believes that it is acting freely under its own volition, ignorant that the law of cause and effect is ceaselessly working through it. Consciousness, entrapped by the 'self', is unable to attain self-awakening.

Couples Bound By Past Karma

The first category of coupling is between people who unconsciously follow the karma of their past relationships to come together again. Because this coupling is based in attachment to the 'self', it is often plagued with trouble and unhappiness.

In fact, I have discovered that many troubled couples were not lovers in their former lives but enemies. In extreme cases, one partner may have even murdered the other. The person who was killed is motivated by revenge, and by marrying their killer they are in a position to do the most damage. The story of my own parents' karma illustrates this point.

My father died of liver cancer in 1973. He worked as the postmaster of Takamatsu City, a city on the Island of Shikoku. He was also president of the Kagawa Prefecture Postmasters' Association. During the year preceding his death he was awarded an Imperial decoration for his many long years of public service. Overjoyed at the honour, he came up to Tokyo to receive the award and was received at the Imperial Court. As a minor official in the Ministry of Postal Services, my father was quite overcome by the opportunity to be in the same room as the Emperor himself. On his way home, he came to visit me and happily described the experience.

In April of the next year I went to lecture in Osaka and met my father again. He didn't appear well to me, and I noticed that he had an unusually poor appetite. He died two months later.

My parents had a horrendous relationship which ended in divorce when I was a child. During the period after the divorce, after my mother joined up with Odaisama, my father continued to abuse her unmercifully. I still have frightful memories of the bloodshed that occurred between them when I was young. Even after my mother came to live with Odaisama at the Shrine in Tokyo, my father's second wife managed to cause a lot of trouble for her.

My mother was seemingly innocent. Why did she have to suffer such cruelty from my father? I have come to realize over the years that these situations are not arbitrary. There is a concrete reason hidden in the past.

My mother has deep faith in God and understands karma. She began to realize that she must have done something
horrible to my father in the past, and decided to undertake
an intensive 100-day period of prayer and asceticism to try
to purify the karma and thus to help my father, herself, and
their descendants. She began her prayers in March. It was
in April that I noticed that my father was ill.

During this time, the story of my parents' karma was
revealed to Odaisama during her daily meditations. It goes
like this:

During the reign of Empress Jingu (AD 201-269), my
mother was a man who served as the Empress's Minister of
State. This was during the time that the Empress was trying
to assimilate Korea. My father was an ambassadorial envoy
from the ancient Korean state of Bekje, who was devoted to
bringing Korean artisans, such as weavers and stone-
masons, to Japan to teach the more highly-developed
Korean techniques. He also used his influence to work for a
peaceful solution to the two countries' political problems.
The ambassador was well received at the Imperial Court,
and he lived there for many years. Unfortunately, he
learned too much about the inner workings of the government and the general opinion was that he had become a
threat to national security and would have to be eliminated.
The Empress herself felt that, in gratitude for his aid, the
ambassador's life should be spared and he should simply be
sent back to Korea. However, the Minister of State (my
present mother) decided that the man posed too great a
threat and, for the sake of Japan and the Imperial House,
took it upon himself to murder the ambassador.

The past karma clearly explains the present situation. In
June of the year my father died, I had a lecture in Shikoku,
where he lived. He was very sick – he had developed
abdominal dropsy and his belly was swollen. After talking to
the doctor I realized that he had only a few days left to live.

I confronted my father and asked him if he was afraid to
die. He admitted that he was very much afraid. I gave him a
sacred amulet and told him that if he clutched it tightly and

thought only of God during death that everything would be all right. I tried to explain that it is crucially important where one directs one's energies at the time of death. If one directs oneself wholeheartedly to God, one will go to God. If one mentally clutches onto someone here on earth, his soul will attach to that person and won't be able to progress easily to the next dimension. It is important to just let go. My father listened attentively and finally nodded in apparent understanding.

As I looked at my father's face I realized that I was seeing him for the last time. I began directing spiritual energy to his cancer. Next morning all the water emptied from his belly. My father pretended to take this as a sign that he was getting better, but I think he knew that he was going to die.

My father passed away the following day, the day of the completion of my mother's hundred days of prayer.

It was as if my father had been ready to die but was unable to do so until my mother helped to dissolve the karma between them. The details of our births and deaths are closely linked to past events. And when a certain karmic knot demands to be dissolved, it has the power to stave off even death.

Another type of couple bound by negative karma are people who had bad marriages in former lives, often plagued with adultery and hatred. They meet, marry, and their trouble begins again. They have the tendency to continue their futile and unending battles, which often span many lifetimes. Outsiders wonder what could possibly be holding the two of them together.

Actually, although it appears painful, it is usually best for this type of couple to be together because it is an opportunity for them to dissolve and expend the negative karma between them. A specific karma is not a limitless entity – once it begins to manifest it will run its course. It is like the carbonation stored in a bottle of soda – there is a 'pop' when you take off the cap, then the fizz wears itself out over time. So it's fine to tackle negative relationships when you realize this principle and are ready to actively work at dissolving past karma. You do this by letting karma run its course and not allowing yourself to repeat the same patterns to create even more of the same negative karma.

Usually this working out is initiated by one of the partners and the other is resistant. As the one partner begins to work towards the dissolution of the karma, the other person may begin to feel even more trapped than before and greatly resist the process. If you are the initiator, at this juncture it is very important to persevere with great determination until the fizz naturally begins to exhaust itself. It is important to realize that you are working not only for yourself but also for the freedom of the other person. If you work wholeheartedly with the aim of releasing both of you, you have the opportunity to transcend your own ego and purely personal considerations. You gain the ability to see things from the other's perspective. And, I assure you, the negative karma will dissolve. Sincere prayer is an effective way to speed your release.

Also in this marital category are many happy couples who are bound together by very positive karma from the past. Good things usually begin to happen to them as soon as they find each other again, in the sense they start getting what they want. These couples have had a long, positive association with each other and have, in a sense, built up a backlog of good karma which manifests when they meet again.

The danger for this type of couple is to become attached to their fortunate situation. Positive karma, as well as negative, is not a limitless entity. If this couple simply enjoys the fruits of their past without using the opportunity to work towards mutual spiritual development, the good karma will just peter out. The more attached they are to the continuation of their happiness, the further they move from God. The reason, again, is because their bonding is grounded in the principle of 'self' attachment. The more one cherishes the 'self', the less one is able to put oneself in the position of the 'other'. One acts only to further the 'self'. As this behaviour continues, what started out as good karma becomes negative. It is best, in this situation, to accept the relationship joyfully but without attachment and to use it as an opportunity to work towards mutual spiritual growth.

Couples bound in the causal dimension

The next category is a type of spiritual bonding. It is when two people are able to connect in the causal dimension, in their 'higher selves'.

The causal self is the self which has 'wholeness and purity of the heart of an infant'. It remains in the immaculate condition in which it was received from God. So the connection on this level between two people is pure and positive. It is comfortable and relaxing just to be around this type of couple: their good feeling has the power to calm negative vibrations around them. These couples tend to remarry over many lifetimes.

A couple bound together in the causal dimension seem to get along effortlessly. Their love brings them out of their own small egos, and they are always able to put themselves in each other's place; each can see from the other's perspective as clearly as they can see from their own. If these two people are able to expand their ability to 'be as the other' into the outside world, they will make rapid spiritual progress. However, their pure interaction is sometimes confined to the marriage and does not extend to other people. Spiritual progress can be made, but more slowly. If their relationship as a married couple continues over many lifetimes, their chances of transcending the world of karma into the higher dimensions are greater than most other types of couples.

Couples as manifest divinity

The most spiritual type of coupling happens as a manifestation of being from the Divine realm.

A unified entity from the divine dimension (beyond causal) can descend to earth as two individuals who then may express their connection in a variety of ways, such as

47

teacher and disciple or parent and child. However, most often they connect here as husband and wife. Such people are truly born to be married to each other. Together they can do great work in the world, expanding the knowledge and consciousness of those around them and helping to lead civilization towards peace and harmony.

In India, China, and Japan there is a widely worshipped Deity known as Avalokitesvara (Kuan-yin, Kannon), the God or Goddess of Compassion. The statues of Avalokitesvara are universally androgynous in that the body is softly curved like a woman, yet the figure has no breasts. This is a representation of the idea that Avalokitesvara exists in a divine dimension of reality where yin and yang, male and female, are unified and undifferentiated. This is a dimension where manifestation does exist but not to the point of individuality, thus differentiating it from the causal dimension.

This type of couple is very rare but it does exist. Because such a couple possesses a shared karma and is bound together in a dimension which itself transcends sexual distinction and individuality, they are one in body and spirit. They most often die about the same time as each other.

Couples bound by physical passion

The fourth category of coupling is that in which two people connect on a purely physical basis. Such couples do not have any karma from past lives influencing them to marry here on earth. They are brought together by sexual, physical passion, the most materialistic of human characteristics.

A physical relationship is an extremely temporary bonding because it does not have the spiritual, mental, and karmic grounding of the other types. We see much of this type of relationship in the modern world, and its temporariness is demonstrated by the consequent high rate of divorce. The transient nature of physical bonding is disturbing because it is nihilistic. Human flesh doesn't last

100 years, so all connections that have the flesh as their main cause are necessarily ephemeral. The more such temporary, ephemeral connections increase, the closer our world moves towards decadence and degeneration.

Couples bound by faith

There is one last category of bonding. It is rare but important, because it is another, but positive, example of bonding that can occur when there is no karma to create it.

If there are two individuals who live in a state of profound faith, God may intercede on their behalf to bring them together. This can happen even if they are in no way karmically related – their faith is all that they share. Their connection is possible, again, because the phenomenon of bonding has its ultimate source in the fact that we all share Divine origin. All variations spring from this common source.

This couple represents a new karmic entity. Once they are brought together they begin to sow the seeds of new karma. They evidence the fact that not everything is controlled by karma. Human beings can create situations into which God will intercede to produce connections which have not existed before. We do not always have to be slaves to karma. True creation and freedom are possible, when we learn how to live in the world of karma without sinking into it.

Every moment of life provides us with two choices: to blindly follow the dictates of past karma or create new karma. It is possible to create new karma when you evolve into the dimensions that transcend karma, if you live your life in close relationship to God.

Sexual karma, that which brings the male and female together, is very basic and very strong. But sexual differentiation itself is not that important – whether you are a man or woman is really no big deal. Your causal body is sexless. Sometimes you incarnate in the physical body of a man and sometimes of a woman. The main factor that determines which it will be is the overriding nature of the attachment that you are experiencing at that point in time. Viewed both karmically and psychologically, attachment to human relationships is more dominantly a female trait and attachment to outside work is more dominantly a male trait, although both sexes possess each type of attachment. Accordingly, a person who is deeply attached to human relationships is likely to be born as a woman and vice versa.

Ultimately, though, male and female distinction is meaningless. There is even a fish, the Cleaner Wrasse (*Labroides dimidiatus*) of Australia's Great Barrier Reef that is naturally equipped with the ability to undergo a sex change. If you isolate a number of Wrasse females together, the dominant member will actually turn into a male. When this male dies, another fish will turn into a male and take his place, thus ensuring progeny.

Among mammals, all sexual differentiation begins with the basic female patterning. Only with the introduction of a special protein which acts to create the testicles does the male of the species appear. This principle can be seen in physics as well. If one side of a slow conducting material is electrolyzed with a strong minus potential, a plus potential will occur on the other side. When a neutral matter is charged with electricity, the polarization of plus and minus occurs.

The occurrence of yin and yang is a principle of nature, and it is necessary to recognize the workings of the principle as it manifests in actual phenomena. For human beings and human karma, however, the actions and attachments of past lives that determine the sex and situation of a person in the present life are more important than the sexual difference itself.

Male and female bind together in the various ways described above. Their commitment to each other, on whatever level they are connected, is a great opportunity for them to dissolve karma. This is a very important fact of life for most people. So much so that one of the ten precepts of the Tamamitsu Shrine is: When marital harmony is achieved, success in all things follows.

This precept reflects the premise that the original root of all marital coupling lies within the pre-differentiated state where we are all one. The most important thing a couple can do is recognize their basic oneness. A way to achieve this is to always put their 'self' completely in the 'other' position – to try to see any situation from the 'other' perspective. To do this, one must be able to break through the narrow confines of the 'self', and this breaking through is what engenders evolution and transcendence. This is true regardless of the level upon which two people are connected.

Too many men and women view each other as objects. When a wife treats her husband as nothing more than a pet dog who carries home a monthly salary cheque in his teeth, this is not a happy bond. The wife has nothing but her own 'self' and her chances of dissolving karma are dim. In the same way, a man who treats his wife as a mere housekeeper is not in a position to create a true marriage connection linked by positive karma.

The word 'harmony' in the Precept above implies the balance of two separate entities, but, in truth, these seemingly distinct entities gradually unify into oneness. When the limiting shell of the 'self' is transcended and cast off, original unity is again possible. If two are able to attain such unity, they are moving closer to the level of the Divine. And, if this level is reached, all things are possible. I think that this is what the precept means.

From personal experience as well as observation, I know how difficult marital harmony is to achieve. But it is possible, and I know many couples who have received direct help from the higher dimensions when they have sincerely committed themselves to spiritual growth.

Family Karma

The family has been the basic unit of society for countless generations. A family is not a chance entity. Its members have normally known each other before, often many times.

Individual members may have been related to each other in any number of ways, from the most positive to the most negative.

Blood is truly thicker than water. A couple may separate and become unrelated, but blood relationships continue until death. Within the web of a familial relationship, the parent/child bond is the strongest. In fact, the relationship between parent and child is often the strongest karma affecting a person in a given lifetime.

The parent/child connection manifests as one link in a long chain of ancestral karma that stretches back through time. Your link to your family allows you to be born into that specific line – it is a link that needs to be understood and respected. In this modern scientific age it is very difficult for people to accept the fact that they are responsible to their ancestors, that they are actually liable for the actions of their ancestors if the resulting karma has not yet been dissolved. Many find it absurd to think that the actions of an unknown ancestor could possibly have anything to do with what is happening to them today. But time and time again, when investigating someone's karma, I find problems that stretch back generations. Their spirit is not just an individual entity, it is also part of the family spirit that births and nurtures it.

Here is an example that illustrates how people tend to be reborn into a given family:

A member of our International Association for Religious Psychology, Mr U., is one of the head priests of the Tenri religion here in Japan. The Tenri religion was founded by a woman named Miki Nakayama in 1938, during a period when Japan was experiencing a huge religious movement that gave birth to many new sects. The Tenri Church has endured and prospered, and now has over 2,500,000 members.

A number of years ago, Mr U. brought a woman psychic to a retreat I was leading at Nebukawa. Apparently, the woman claimed that Miki Nakayama was manifesting through her. Mr U. asked me to confirm whether her claim was true or not. If she truly was channelling Miki Nakayama it would have profound implications for the church.

I examined the woman, and I clearly saw that two souls were attached to her. One was the spirit of a woman who was in her thirties who told me her name was Yasu. The other was the spirit of a woman in her mid-fifties named Sayo. Reverend Nakayama was nowhere to be found. It turns out, however, that both of these spirits had been Miki Nakayama's daughters and it was they who were influencing the psychic. Here is their story:

Reverend Nakayama bore six children during her lifetime, all of whom, except the eldest, were female. The name of her second daughter was Yasu. Yasu died when she was three years old. At that time, apparently, the Nakayama family was entrusted with the care of a child from another family. This child contracted smallpox. Reverend Nakayama was so distraught that she had failed in her duty to the child's family that she fervently begged God to make the child well, whatever the cost. The child recovered but Miki's own three year old Yasu was taken from her. In her grief, the Reverend had a vision that Yasu would be reborn in three years' time as a girl named Tsune, that the child Tsune would die three years after her birth, and that finally, the soul would be born as another child to be named Kokan.

The prophecy was fulfilled. Kokan was born as Rev Nakayama's youngest daughter, after the death of Tsune. Kokan was a woman of great faith, and her mother planned to appoint her as her successor. The Reverend sent Kokan to open a branch of the church in Osaka, and Kokan devoted herself wholeheartedly to the project. Kokan had been appointed to remain single and to devote herself to the propagation of the Tenri religion, but she suddenly fell in love when she was thirty-nine and decided to get married. Rev Nakayama received the urgent prophecy that if Kokan married, it would quickly end in disaster, and that she would return to her family and soon after die.

Despite her mother's adamant protestations, Kokan stubbornly refused to obey the prophecy. She went ahead and got married anyway. A week after the wedding she returned, utterly dejected, to her mother's house. Two weeks later she died.

It is interesting that the spirit I saw had the name of Yasu but was in her thirties. We see here a combination of astrally manifested facets of one single soul. The soul was born first as Yasu, died at three, was born again in Tsune, died again at three, and was finally born as Kokan and died at thirty-nine. So the thirtyish Yasu I saw was the same soul in the form she had last died in at thirty-nine.

Reverend Nakayama's third daughter was named Haru. She married into the Kajimoto family and died in 1873 at the age of forty-two. At the time of Haru's death, Miki received the prophecy that this daughter would be reborn as a female into a family named Yamazawa and that she would again marry into the Kajimoto family. Sixteen years later, in 1889, the Yamazawa family gave birth to a girl child who they named Sayo. She grew up to marry into the Kajimoto family. Sayo was an ardent devotee of Tenri and became so respected in the organization that following her death, at 50, she was enshrined in the church. The spirit of Sayo is the other spirit I encountered at the class in Nebukawa.

One interesting thing about Sayo is that she married into the same family in two different incarnations. When you begin to understand the machinations of karma, you realize how important it is to treat your family well. Your daughter-in-law may have previously been a daughter of your own house, your grandson's wife may have been your own daughter. The possibilities are endless.

One of our Shrine members, Mr M., asked for a spiritual consultation a few months before his first grandchild was born. During the consultation a spirit appeared before me, and I could discern that it was the spirit of Mr M.'s second son who had been born in 1932 and died in 1939 at the age of seven. The young spirit spoke to me in a childish voice and said, 'I'm so happy. Something wonderful is going to happen, but I'm not allowed to tell anybody about it yet.'

I then had a clairvoyant vision of Mr M., all dressed up in formal wear, holding a boy child in his arms and presenting him at the Shrine. I realized at this point that the spirit of Mr M.'s second son was about to be reborn as his own grandson.

The grandson was born and is now grown. He has always been very close to and taken very good care of his grandfather. Even when he went through his rebellious stages, he would quickly do whatever his grandfather asked of him. Mr M. derived great joy from the boy. This is a clear example of mutual care and support, and is a good example of how families can function. Mr M. is very religious, and after his son died he took great care to honour and respect him. It is important to take good care of one's relations, in death as well as life.

People come into a family, whether through birth or marriage, because they have the karma to do so, and, chances are, they have been related by blood to the same individuals in previous lives. This is because people who have worked together as a family unit often have the karma to gather together again.

The semi-tropical and temperate areas of Asia, including Southeast Asia, Korea, and parts of China, have been predominantly agrarian for thousands of years. Many families have tilled the same soil for generations. In a farming family, survival depends upon the labour of every member, including the children. This often results in very strong family bonds, where the family soul exerts strong control over the affairs of the family members for hundreds of years.

In Japan, as in these other countries, we have a tradition of ancestor worship. Family lines are closely protected, and many families can trace their exact linkage back over fifteen or twenty generations. When someone dies, he or she receives a posthumous name that is inscribed on a memorial tablet. Many people place these tablets on the family altar in their homes, and honour them every day. We also have a number of festivals that honour the souls of the dead.

The deeds of an ancestor can create family karma that continues to influence the fate of the family's descendants until the karma is dissolved. For instance, a Ms O. came to ask me for a spiritual consultation because her family's shipping business was in a serious slump. I entered samadhi and with my inner eye saw a large sailing ship that was just about to sink. It was about 80 years ago. The ship's mast had been broken in a storm in the Inland Sea. At the foot of the mast, a young sailor was lying dead at the end of an exhausted effort to save the ship.

I became aware that the captain of the ship, who was Ms O.'s grandfather, was responsible for this tragic accident. He had insisted on sailing with a full load even though bad weather was predicted. The young sailor had pleaded with the captain not to leave port. He was not heeded. He died bearing a grudge against the captain, and this was the cause of the curse on the family.

When I spoke to Ms O., I asked her if any other of their ships had been sunk at sea. They certainly had. Twice. One was a ship weighing 300 tons, the other weighed 500.

The results of her grandfather's actions were serious because they involved other people's lives. The family karma that resulted was still in effect today. I advised Ms O. to devote heartfelt prayers to the unfortunate young sailor for a period of 200 days, until his suffering soul was liberated. The family shipping business then began to gradually improve and is now very successful.

Conversely, I have seen many people who are suffering present-day problems as a result of angering the spirits of their ancestors. One man came to me because he and his family were suffering terribly from a variety of psychological and emotional problems. The problems started soon after he accepted a high-ranking position in one of Japan's new religions. Upon psychic investigation, I found out that they had donated a large amount of land and other property that had been in his family for generations to the church. He was not a particularly able man and, in effect, had sold his birthright to obtain a position of prominence.

The spirit of the former head of the family, the man who had acquired the property and amassed the original fortune, was outraged by the sudden loss of wealth. He was venting his rage on the man and other members of the living family, causing them to suffer the problems they were experiencing.

Some of these new religions do wreak havoc with the past. I know of one sect where members are required to 'start a new life' by 'giving up their past'. They do this by giving their family's memorial tablets to the church. The church gives these tablets as well as those of other new members to someone of relative authority, like a chapter head or group leader. He proceeds to line all of the tablets on his own family's altar and begins daily prayer before them.

A stranger has just taken on the burden of praying for a lot of unknown souls. This is a potentially dangerous situation. If the person is sufficiently evolved spiritually, he or she will be able to help the souls being prayed for. And if the souls themselves are well on their way to obtaining Buddhahood, there will be no problem. The evolving souls will just be grateful for the prayers and no harm will be done. Problems do arise, however, when the souls exist in a state of suffering. They attach to the prayers in hopes of gaining some release and become dependent on the individual who is praying for them. The greater the suffering, the greater the dependency. The human being will be adversely affected by the suffering he is calling onto himself through his prayers.

Even though praying for others' souls is basically a noble deed, this person is way out of his depth; he is trying to save a bunch of drowning people when he can't swim himself. The whole bunch may all end up going under. He would probably get very sick. I doubt he would die; help will eventually come from higher sources because the nature of his deeds is well-meaning and positive. But in the meantime, he and his family members would have experienced needless suffering.

Imagine this scene from the other side. The human being starts praying for other families' ancestors as well as his own. This is just like he has invited a gang of parasitic strangers to live with his ancestors under the same roof. Naturally, the ancestors get angry, which only contributes to an already volatile situation.

The karma of your ancestors and your family line is not limitless. Like all other karma, it will eventually come to an end – the family line will disappear. People often fight this reality and go to great lengths to ensure that their family name continues. In Japan, if a family has no male heir they find a suitable husband for their eldest daughter and adopt him. The husband takes the wife's surname and legally becomes the next Head-of-Household. This is still common practice.

Through spiritual consultations, however, I have found that this is not always the wisest course of action. In particular, when a family bears females only for a number of generations it is a sign that the family is destined to die out.

Family lines may be destined to end as a result of negative karma accumulated in the past. One specific case I have seen is one in which an ancestor, in his effort to establish and ensure the prosperity of his own lineage, usurped another family's property and annihilated that household in the process. His intense attachment to his own family line has left a karmic trail behind him.

Other cases of the end of a line are often the result of entangled sexual desire. This is particularly true when a former generation was polygamous. The disharmony in a household where there were a number of wives or concubines can cause present-day confusion. The conflicts which arose between these women may continue to plague a family for generations. When people come to me who are unknowingly burdened with such a history, they usually report stories of family trouble in their parents' and grandparents' generations. If such negative karma is not dissolved, the family line most usually comes to an end.

In our own lives, the relationships we invariably need to do a lot of work with are to our parents and our children.

Often the parent/child relationship is a deeply positive one. I was surprised when I first began doing spiritual consultations at how often the people in a truly happy parent/child bond had been lovingly compatible couples in a former incarnation. This is also sometimes the case between a close brother and sister. And of course, I often find that a happy parent and child have been in the same relationship before. Or that their roles have been reversed. Just by being together here again these two people are able to dissolve karma and to deal successfully with the outside world.

The parent/child bond may also be intensely negative. The media sadly brings our attention to an appalling incidence of child abuse and, conversely, to parent abuse and neglect of the aged. The crimes of infanticide and patricide go beyond the boundaries of common understanding yet they do occur. I cannot give you a general karmic cause for all of this suffering; each case would have to be dealt with separately in terms of past history. But it is safe to conclude that whatever binds this kind of parent and child together is extreme and very deep.

In either case, the karma between parent and child is usually the most difficult the individual has to dissolve. It follows that if one is able to dissolve such deep karmic connections one makes great progress towards freedom and Enlightenment. It is important, therefore, that we try.

It is difficult to dissolve the karma between parent and child because the connection is so intimate and the attachment so great. Intense emotions are involved. People easily make sacrifices for their children that they wouldn't think of doing for another human being. A loving parent truly rejoices in a child's success, and palpably suffers at his sorrow. But it is often impossible for a parent to escape the role of mother or father. It is very hard for a parent to view an offspring as anything other than a child, and for the child to let go of the parent as parent. This inability to view each other as human beings is why the karma between the two is so difficult to dissolve.

If one is able to undo the knots of attachment that bind one to his or her parents and children in this life, one accomplishes great work. I will deal at length with the topic of how one dissolves karma in a later chapter, but first let us turn our attention to other kinds of karma.

CHAPTER FOUR

The Varieties of Karma: National, Racial and Geographic Karma

The next three types of karma I wish to discuss – national, racial, and geographic karma – are more or less tightly interwoven in the life of any single individual. They are intimately related to family karma as well.

National Karma

When we look at a country using the physical eye we can see only its physical characteristics. When we look at the country of Japan we see an entity composed of four major islands that contain mountains, rivers, and vegetation and that are surrounded by ocean. Nature took many millennia to create this place. She used earthquakes, volcanoes, a whole array of geographic phenomena to sculpt this land into what it is today. Most of this work took place before the birth of man.

But when I look at Japan using non-physical perception, I see a very different picture. Rather than mountains and rivers, I see a vast underlying Spirit. This is the Spiritual Existence of the country which enabled the land itself to materialize on the physical plane. The ancient Japanese people perceived the presence of this Spiritual Existence and sanctified it as the National Deity.

Each nation on earth has its own Spirit, and that Spirit has its own karma. Spirit exists before matter, and the National Spirit is what causes the land formation to generate. It then acts as the agent of materialization for the living things born to that land and the eventual emergence of human beings. The karma of the National Spirit affects everyone living in

---

the country, whether they are born there or immigrate from other places.

During normal times we are free to act out our individual karmic dramas while living on any given national soil. In states of national emergency such as wartime, however, most individuals become as powerless before the state a꜡ ants before an oncoming steamroller. This is true of any situation in which a large proportion of the populace meets with death at the same time: war, famine, plague, and is due to the fact, simply, that the National Spirit is incomparably larger than that of an individual human being. Most people, therefore, become subsumed in any major manifestation of National karma occurring around them. Yet there are always a few individuals who manage to stay distinct and survive a national crisis, no matter how far-reaching. They might have a backlog of better karma than their neighbours, or maybe God has selected to use them for some purpose.

I am reminded of the tremendous defeat that Japan suffered in World War II, after a history of never having been conquered or defeated by a foreign power. I think that our National Deity was reaping the harvest of seeds it had sown in the past. And observing the seeds that Japan is now sowing in its present state of prosperity, I feel concern for the potential karmic shoots of the future.

Wherever you were born, it is important to recognize the karma that binds you to your country and treat it with respect. The Japanese may possess an extreme inclination towards obstinate loyalty and patriotism, but that is their karma and they must work through it.

I feel that it is important to work first for the prosperity of one's own country and its people, and then to work for the peace and prosperity of other peoples. One who tries to promote world peace but who has no roots is like a cut flower standing in a vase – he or she will soon wither. If you are unconcerned about your own country but assume the airs of a globally-minded person, little will come of your efforts. It seems that it is important to breathe fully the energy of your land and its people in order to be able to transcend national distinctions, begin significant interaction with other peoples of the world, and become a truly international person. Grass without roots cannot grow.

Racial Karma

Racial karma is another powerful category of karma. It is that which brings each race into being. There are great variations in the degree that National and Racial karma are connected and manifest. I had an interesting experience in the United States that helps to illustrate this point.

Some years ago I accepted the invitation of an American disciple of mine to visit the town of Mendacino on the northern coast of California. He had opened a yoga centre there and was teaching about 200 people.

The surrounding area is Redwood country – dense forests of ancient cedar trees, some 3000 years old. The people I met there were mostly lumberjacks, living a fairly communal lifestyle. They were all white people, mostly of Russian or English descent. The environment was majestic and peaceful, yet I felt an underlying unrest and conflict in these people that I didn't immediately understand.

The first night there I slept in a small hut in the middle of the forest. In my dreams I was surrounded by the spirits of Native American Indians who used to populate the area. They had all been murdered by settlers and were collectively carrying a ferocious animosity towards white people, especially Russians. In the continuing vision, I saw that many of this group had been, and were presently being born as Caucasians. It was clear that the group of people I had just met was largely comprised of such beings and that this was the root of their confusion.

The people were now white on the outside but more Indian on the inside – no wonder there was a cultural identity problem. Their way of thinking and the lifestyle they had chosen bore more resemblance to their Indian past than to the contemporary American present. They collectively carried the guilt of having murdered their former selves.

The next day, during a workshop, I spoke to a woman's liberation activist who told me she had had the realization that she had been an American Indian in a former life. I then asked my disciple to check into the historical records of settlement in the area. Indeed, he verified that the majority of white people who settled Mendacino were Russians who destroyed the local Indian population.

In the case of a huge, diversified country like the United States, the National Spirit is not identical with the Spirit of any one race. The National Spirit can manifest in various racial forms, and these Racial Spirits are subsidiary to the National Karma. For many centuries the National Spirit of the country we call the United States caused the birth of Indians onto the land and protected their existence. Then over the last few hundred years, the National Spirit allowed the immigration of European and other races to American soil. It has ensured their prosperity under the dictates of the National Karma. The Soviet Union is an example of another country where the National Karma is much more powerful than that of any one race.

In contrast there are small insulated countries like Japan and Germany, where the National Spirit and the Racial Spirit are almost identical. This identity empowers the Racial Spirit, which results in the national characteristic of attachment to racial purity. In Germany this trait has been enforced by the years of disputes it had with its many contiguous neighbours. In Japan the trait has become firmly entrenched because we are an isolationist, island country. The Japanese race is like an only child which has had an overprotective upbringing.

Because the Spirit of the Nation and Race are so strong, the percentage of Japanese who are reborn into other countries is small. The karmic interlocking of generations of Japanese being born here time and again is at the basis of our homogeneity. In spiritual consultations, however, I have encountered a number of Japanese who were either Chinese or Korean in former times. This happens because Japan has had diplomatic relations with these countries and they are racially similar. And, of course, I have also met karmically freer spirits whose births cross all national and racial boundaries.

So if a Japanese couple goes to the United States and gives birth to a child whom they raise there, is the child Japanese or American? We assume, legally and otherwise, that the child is still pure Japanese, but I question this. The child's spirit will be directly affected by living on American soil under the dictates of the American National Spirit.

As for myself, I was first born in Japan about 3500 years ago and have had a number of incarnations here as well as in other places. Before my first incarnation here I lived in China, where my interest in medicine has continued in my present-day research in acupuncture and the meridian systems. I have had intermittent lifetimes in India, Greece, and Europe. But I feel I have lived in Japan enough times now, and expect that this is my farewell encounter with this country. I expect to be born in a larger, more diversified country the next time around.

Most Japanese people, however, will continue to be re-born here. The identification of National and Racial Karma acts as an obstruction to an individual being reborn in another country or into another race. We are not the only race, of course, to exhibit this tendency; all countries and races have it to a certain extent.

It is clear, though, that the Japanese National Spirit exerts a stronger control over each individual soul here than the National Spirit does in most other countries. Individual egos here are weak, people have difficulty demonstrating their abilities when acting alone. We have what the sociologists always refer to as 'group consciousness'. In the West, the individual is central, whereas in Japan a person deals with the outside world as a member of the group to which he or she belongs. When you meet a Japanese businessman he introduces himself by giving his company name before his own. His loyalty to his group resembles that of a dog to his master. I feel this has distinct disadvantages, but it does mean that Japanese can change their course of action very quickly and are able to act with foresight unclouded by individual opinion.

One people whose Racial Spirit and National Spirit have a very distinct relationship is the Jewish people. The Jewish people are directly descended from the first Homo Sapiens who appeared in what is now the northwest part of India and Iran about one hundred thousand years ago. Due to climatic changes, these people were made to scatter in all directions. The ancestors of the Jew settled in Canaan in Israel sometime between ten and thirty thousand years ago. After that time they were made to move to other places – to Mesopotamia, and to Egypt as slaves. After the Crucifixion of Jesus, the Jews lost control of their country and became a wandering race scattered all over the world. This has been the karma of the Jews from ancient times. However, their elitism, pride, and unity in their faith never died or declined. This firmness finally resulted in the establishment of their own country after the Second World War. The Jews are clear evidence that National Spirit and Racial Spirit do not necessarily coincide with one another. A Racial Spirit can exist without its own National Spirit.

Geographic Karma

The planet Earth is the material manifestation of the Planetary Spirit. This translates to mean that all natural objects and all geographic locations are imbued with their own spirit. Ancient people knew this fact; modern man has forgotten it. It is misguided to think that we can do whatever we want to the nature around us. Earth, stones, trees, tiny insects, all of the things that live together on this planet have spirit.

The following story illustrates what happened when one family offended a natural Spirit, in this case the Water Spirit.

A woman came to me beset with various problems. Her second husband had just died. She was suffering from a bad case of asthma and many of her relatives had suddenly got sick. Their complaints ranged from tuberculosis to heart disease to mental illness. Lately they had all been fighting with each other. She could no longer believe that the situation was coincidental and had come seeking karmic reasons behind the situation.

When I went into samadhi I saw a large estate on which there were many wells. I saw that the estate had been in this woman's family for many years. The family had been prosperous sake distillers, a very respected position in traditional Japanese society. They were able to produce an excellent product because of the purity of the water that was so abundant on their land. In fact, the water had been sustaining the wealth and security of the family for generations.

It turns out that the distillery had been closed down by her father's generation. The estate lay quiet. Then this woman, along with the rest of the family, decided to build an apartment complex on the estate. They simply bulldozed all the wells out of existence.

I saw that the Water Spirit was understandably outraged and was retaliating by causing the family its present problems. They had acted selfishly for their own profit, with no thought of apology or thanksgiving to the Water Spirit of the wells.

Accordingly, I directed the woman before me to offer daily prayers of apology and thanksgiving and to chant certain sutras to the Spirit of Water. During the prescribed period, her asthma disappeared, everyone in the family recovered, and the general mood of the household improved tremendously. Her prayers were even more effective than initially intended. Apparently one of her tenants living in an apartment built directly over one of the wells had been very ill. The tenant recovered completely as well.

In a long-standing traditional society such as ours, land karma and family karma tend to be intimately connected. As a long-time agrarian society, many families still possess land that they have lived on for generations. I sometimes only have to ask a consultee where they were born, and their family and individual karmic history immediately unfolds before me.

I had a similar experience with an Indian woman who was visiting the Institute from Bombay. She is the trustee of a medical college and came to discuss the idea of incorporating acupuncture together with Ayurvedic treatment as preventive medicine into her organization. She was also experiencing some medical problems and was seeking relief through acupuncture treatment. Upon examining her, I realized that she needed a spiritual consultation as well, because the cause of her problems did not lie in the physical dimension.

Upon entering meditation in the Shrine, I saw the spirit of her deceased mother-in-law. The spirit was not yet liberated from this world and was still suffering. She needed help from her daughter-in-law to become free. I also saw the image of a huge old tree in a garden. The tree was next to the woman's house. There was a spirit in the tree that was protecting the surrounding area. The tree was casting so much shade and producing so many fallen leaves that the woman's neighbours wanted to cut it down. She alone had been fighting against that decision. I could see that the Spirit of the tree was grieving about its impending doom. Both of these spirits were affecting the woman's health.

When I related to her what I had seen, this woman said that her physical condition had begun to deteriorate soon after her mother-in-law's death. I advised her to pray for her mother-in-law with a trustworthy priest of the Jain religion, of which she is a member. They needed to help the spirit understand that everything in this world is transient and that the way to liberation is to direct the mind to the Absolute.

As for the tree, she was worried that her neighbours would cut it down in her absence. I advised her to ask her neighbours not to do so. She called India and was surprised to learn that the tree had been felled the night before by a cyclone. I advised her to plant a new tree of the same yang type on the same spot so that the Spirit protecting that area could live there again.

People who recognize the divinity of nature do not act carelessly. Mr K. is a member of the Shrine who has this understanding. He is the president of a large corporation that is presently constructing a new building. Mr K. took time out from his hectic schedule to come and see me the other day; he had just found out that there was a huge well on the building site and that a woman had drowned herself in it fifty years ago after a fight with her elder brother. He wanted to know if it was okay to demolish the well or if he should leave it alone. I advised him to pray that the spirit of the woman be freed from her pain and to offer ritual thanks to the Water Spirit who sustained the people of the area. I told him that the well should not be completely buried and that the area above it should not be used for some polluting purpose like a toilet. Contact was maintained between the well and the outside world by means of a small pipe. Mr K. built a small shrine on the site dedicated to the Water Spirit, and the construction is proceeding normally.

Water, like everything else, is more than it appears within the narrow limits of the physical dimension. This explains why ritual offerings of food and water are truly effective ways of helping beings suffering in the astral dimension, particularly the souls of people who have recently died. When we place an offering upon the altar, we don't expect it to disappear because we know that someone who has died cannot eat physical substances. When we expand our field of vision into the higher dimensions, however, we can actually see spirits consuming the offerings. They are consuming the 'ki' of the food and water, the astral energy of the objects that exists even before the object manifests into the physical world.

In the material world we are only able to grasp physical phenomena as they are perceived through the senses. We experience the existence of electricity when it manifests as light. When it is not manifest we are unable to perceive it. There is a monumental power behind physical reality that causes physical phenomena to occur. Certain philosophical systems, such as the Greek and the Hindu, break this power down into fundamental elements and name them earth, water, fire, wind, and air. Each of these elements is much more than a physical phenomenon; each has its own Spirit. The larger Spirit manifests into smaller entities and thus we account for beings such as mountain and water spirits.

The Karma of Place

Places have spirit as well. This became evident to me years ago when I got involved in real estate to generate the funds to establish the Institute for Religious Psychology. Before deciding whether or not to buy a piece of land, I would stand on it and go into meditation to check out the level of spiritual power of the land. This would disclose the potential value of the land. Sure enough, the land I invested in was all included in some rapid development plan, either residential or commercial. In another case, a person came to get my opinion on his decision to locate his business on a certain site. I entered samadhi and attempted to perceive the karma of the land. It appeared to me that the power of the land spirit was weak and the area was subject to negative spiritual influences. I advised him to look for another place. He took my advice and now his business is flourishing. As I expected, the area where he originally proposed to locate his office is far from prosperous.

A physical location may be greatly affected by its karmic history. Events can still be occurring on the astral plane which are not readily apparent on the physical. I got a big dose of this when I established our retreat centre at Nebukawa, southwest of Tokyo.

The land itself is beautiful, high on a hillside overlooking the Pacific Ocean. In the first few years there, while the centre was under construction, I often experienced a great sense of uneasiness, sometimes to the point of nausea, when I meditated while on the site. One day in meditation I saw the following scene:

Two warriors were in a life and death struggle. They were grappling for hours. Night fell and neither had won. They hid from each other and both lay there in a state of complete exhaustion. I identified one of the men as an assistant general in the Genji army named Yoichi Sanada. The other man was a general in the rival Heike army. I then saw a number of Yoichi's retainers appear, searching for him. They stumbled upon him in the dark, and mistaking him for the enemy, brutally stabbed him to death. As mentioned before, the head of the victorious Genji army was Yoritomo Minamoto, who founded the Kamakura shogunate that ruled a unified Japan from 1185 to 1333.

Yoichi had been dead for 800 years, yet his tortured spirit was still able to affect me when I began to build our retreat centre. We began to pray for his soul in the Shrine. After three years of such prayers, his resentment dissolved and I no longer experienced any negativity. I finally felt comfortable enough to bring other Shrine members and yogic meditation students to the Centre.

This case shows how strong the attachment to the place of death can be. Yoichi was not an unmourned soul: for generations his family and his clansmen did all they could for him, even constructing a small shrine in Nebukawa to appease his soul. Yet it still took 800 long years for him to get free.

Something else happened in Nebukawa. As I mentioned, sometimes in those early days I would start feeling seasick during meditation. When I looked clairvoyantly to find the cause of the nausea, I saw an entire train lying at the bottom of the sea. The bodies of the passengers were lying piled up upon one another inside the carriages. I also saw a lot of people who looked like farmers, young and old, buried under the ground and crying out.

I mentioned all of this to the local village headman. He told me that a strange thing happened to the surrounding fields after Yoichi's death. All the root vegetables – the radishes, the carrots, the burdock – came out of the ground twisted. The locals had long ago named the area 'Twisted Fields'.

He told me that the two other scenes were from a terrible tragedy that happened during the Great Kanto Earthquake of 1923. The village of Nebukawa was totally destroyed by a landslide and quite a number of people died under the weight of the earth. At the same time, a railway train that was stopped at Nebukawa station tumbled over the cliffs and into the sea. It is still there today. Upon hearing all this I felt a connection between Yoichi Sanada's spirit and the karma of the old battlefield and the tragedy of 1923.

How, then, did we come to choose such a spiritually polluted place for the site of our yoga retreat?

There is a mountain near Kyoto that is considered one of the holiest places in Japan. Its name is Mt. Koya and it is the headquarters of Shingon Buddhism, a popular esoteric sect. There are hundreds of temples on the mountain, many of which accept pilgrims who wish to do religious retreats. About 30 years ago I was staying at one such temple to give teachings to the leader of a newer religious sect. At that time during my meditation I saw Yoritomo Minamoto and his son Yoriie appear in front of me and give me deep courteous bows. I was merely 30 years old and had had only a few years' experience of concerted spiritual practice at that time, so I didn't quite know how to interpret the vision. Next day I told my vision to the resident priest of the temple. He replied in astonishment that of the hundred or so temples located on Mt. Koya, his temple is the only one in which Yoritomo and Yoriie Minamoto are worshipped. In fact, both of their graves are actually located there. This was interesting information, but still didn't answer my question as to why they had appeared before me.

I discovered the answer 20 years later. I was in the midst of a spiritual consultation for someone else, and in the light of information revealed, realized that I was a figure in the shogunate of their time. I was the one who, at Yoritomo's request, had conferred the post of Shogun to Yoriie as his successor. I understood then why they both had appeared to me on Mt. Koya 30 years before. And why, in a sense, it was my karma to choose Nebukawa so that I could purify the land where Yoritomo raised his army, and where many of his generals and soldiers, including Yoichi Sanada, had died.

The area surrounding Nebukawa has seen much battle activity over the years. As is clear from the many examples, Japan has had a very war-torn history. Here is another experience from the time when we were looking for land on which to build our retreat centre. We were scouting the area around Nebukawa, in the towns of Isehara, Ninomiya, and Odawara. Our Tokyo Shrine had been receiving a lot of media attention, and many people from this area suddenly started showing up at the Shrine for spiritual consultations.

One morning I was meditating as usual in the shrine, and there were ten or so people meditating behind me. The door to the entrance vestibule slid open, and someone entered the Shrine. I sit facing the altar in the inner Shrine, and the other meditators sit behind me, also facing the altar, in the outer shrine, but I am able to see clairvoyantly what is going on in the outer Shrine. The person who entered was a woman. As she bowed down before the altar, I saw a ghastly-looking warrior, wearing a bloody helmet, hovering directly behind her. The abruptness of his gruesome visage surprised me, but I went in for a closer look.

It turns out that the apparition was a samurai of the Takeda Clan who had died on the battlefield. The details gradually became clearer. The beautiful visage of Mt. Oh, the central peak of the Tanzawa chain in Kangawa prefecture, floated before me. I was simultaneously able to see the woman in the Shrine with the spirit of the warrior right behind her right shoulder. Although I have never climbed Mt. Oh, and have only seen it from a distance on the way to Nebukawa, I was able to see then that the foot of Mt. Oh is hilly. Right below the hills is an area of cultivated vegetable fields, rather than the usual wet rice paddies. In one corner of a field I saw a tumulus, then I noticed tumuli scattered here and there over the area. One of the tumuli had been dug open. In a flash I realized that the Takeda warrior hovering in the outer Shrine had been buried in the now defaced grave. I saw that this woman's family home was at the base of Mt. Oh, and that many years ago her father had bought the field containing the tomb in which the samurai's soul was resting and proceeded to dig it up. After this, there was a rise in the number of demented people both in his family and in the surrounding village. I saw that the woman's son was presently being possessed by the spirit of the warrior and that as a result he was suffering severe psychological problems.

When meditation was over, I told the woman, who had not yet said one word to me, everything that I had seen. She was dumbfounded. She finally stammered out a reply, saying that yes, her family home was in Isehara, at the base of Mt. Oh, and that she had heard something about the story. She said that her son had become ill in the third year of Junior High School, and that he was now hospitalized as schizophrenic. She had come to the Shrine seeking consultation about his problem. I explained to her that the karma of the situation was quite deep and couldn't be dissolved instantly, but that I would pray about it over the next week and see what I could do. I then had her go home.

Instead, she rushed off to her family seat in Isehara to ask her elder brother, who was now head of the family, about the tomb. He told her the same story I did. It seems that in the village there had been a family known as the 'family of ruin' because anyone who bought something from them ended up in trouble. The elder brother told his sister that their father had bought the field containing the tumulus from this 'family of ruin'. Because their father was a very stingy man, he dug up the tumulus and made it into a rice paddy. From that time on, a number of people in the family and in the village became psychologically unstable each year. The woman told me all this the next day, and also the fact that when her son first began to become ill he had written in his notebook, 'I am a vassal of the Takeda Clan . . . '. She had had no idea what that meant.

For one week I pleaded with God to forgive and comfort the spirit of the warrior. At the end of the one-week period, the woman returned to the Shrine and with much excitement told me that something extraordinary had happened. Her son had at last been released from the hospital and was functioning well enough to help her out in her store as soon as he returned home. The spirit of the warrior had at last been relieved of his suffering.

When a person dies a violent death, he or she often becomes deeply attached to the terror, suffering, or hatred experienced during the death. This attachment prevents the person from realizing the fact that they are dead, which is normally the first step in continuing his or her journey. Because the person doesn't recognize that they are dead, their state of suffering may continue for hundreds of years.

As mentioned earlier, praying for these people is one way to help them attain the necessary realization. For this reason, each year we hold a service for the unmourned dead at the Shrine in July. Until recently, I always felt a lingering, negative influence from the suffering spirits for days after the service was over, so we decided to place offerings outside the fence of the main Shrine building as a memorial service to those spirits who are too defiled to enter into the shrine precincts. The situation is now improving, and here is what I think is happening.

The Pacific War ended over 40 years ago. Many people died during the conflict in extreme states of anger and terror. Their souls have needed help in rising to the higher levels of consciousness. Many people have since offered earnest prayers to help these spirits. Looking at the situation clairvoyantly, I see that many of the Japanese who died on Japanese soil now appear free. However, some men who died on foreign soil, particularly in the South Pacific, are still locked in a miserable state of suffering. These men met with gruesome deaths like burning and starvation and it is very difficult for them to find release from the intense states of terror and hatred they have remained in all these years.

The stronger the suffering and hatred, the more these beings are frozen to the physical locale where they died. And it has been difficult to help them from a distance. But after years of concerted effort by mostly Shinto religious groups, the spirits stuck in the South Pacific are gradually getting cleaner.

Cleaner may seem like a strange word to use, but it is apt because attachment makes a spirit impure. This impurity has the power to exert a negative influence on the other beings with whom the spirit comes in contact. People who come for spiritual consultations often 'carry' with them such suffering spirits. Sometimes I absorb the influence of the defiled spirits and feel temporarily ill myself.

This phenomenon, commonly called possession, is much more common than most people realize. We 'possess', or attach to, to each other in an endless number of ways. This possession occurs both within and across the dimensions, and is positive or negative depending on the inherent relationship between the two beings.

Recently a stranger who was exuding this type of spiritual negativity came for a consultation. During the morning meditation, before the day of consultations, I saw the roof of a large temple connected to the person, and during the consultation I saw that he had a deep relationship to a certain Shinto Shrine. Due to the influence of a related karma, the man's health was beginning to fail. I petitioned God to dissolve the karma, and the gentleman was purified. I immediately felt released from the negative influence I had been receiving from him. This same purification/release mechanism is why I have been feeling less negative influence after our service for the dead. Many of the defiled souls who were attracted to the Shrine in the past have been purified and need our help no longer.

There are various areas on earth, like former disaster sites and battlefields, that contain an especially large number of suffering spirits. The land there is unclean, they are bad karmic areas. I always caution my students against meditating in such a place, since their heightened psychic vulnerability would make them easy prey for the suffering spirits. These areas are often the sites of accidents, and they are difficult to develop commercially.

Land karma is not only of the bad kind, of course. We are now in the process of enlarging buildings within the Shrine complex. The house next door has also begun some new construction. And a brand new house has just been finished across the street. A certain type of activity in an area tends to attract similar activity. Around the time that Odaisama died, many other old people also died in the surrounding neighbourhood.

Phenomena such as birth, death, and real estate development occur in an area as a result of the cumulative effect of the karma of the place itself and of the individual karma of the people who live there.

I would like to end this section with an elaboration of my parents' karmic story because it illustrates how closely Natural, Geographic, and Family Karma can be linked. Years after we learned that my mother had killed my father in a past life, causing him to abuse her in this one, a more complete and complex history unfolded.

April 8, 1984 was the 30th anniversary of the present construction of the Tamamitsu Shrine in Mitaka, Tokyo. We organized a large ceremonial event, spending months on its preparation. As the event neared, I became seriously ill. Fearing I would not be able to uphold my duties, I performed a spiritual consultation and was given the following information.

Odaisama and I were also high ranking members of the Yamato government when my father was the ambassador from Korea and my mother the Minister of State, as was detailed in 'Couples Bound by Past Karma' in Chapter Three. The government had colonized a state called 'Imhara' in southern Korea and was on friendly terms with Bejke, a country located in the southwest part of Korea. Many powerful and learned families came to Japan during the 5th century from Kudara, introducing advanced technologies to the Japanese people. They brought with them the skill of iron production which spread rapidly throughout society. Large scale public engineering and water supply works were put into operation. They introduced new ways of mass producing ceramics, of breeding livestock, and of manufacturing silk. They also brought with them an advanced knowledge of arithmetic and Chinese characters. In effect, the contributions of the Korean immigrants, through the transmission of so much knowledge from the continent, resulted in a new epoch of civilization in Japan.

At the same time, the Koreans gained a lot of political clout which began to be seen as a threat by the Japanese government. The situation became increasingly tense, then boiled over when the Japanese Minister of State murdered the Korean ambassador. It was felt that the immigrants from Kudara knew too much about Japan to be allowed to return to Korea, so they were summarily exiled to a remote area far from Yamato, the metropolitan centre in that period of history. That remote place is now called Mitaka, and is a part of Tokyo. This area has many place names containing 'Mure' (the word Mure is derived from the ancient Korean word for village).

It turns out that our Shrine complex on the edge of Inokashira Park is located exactly in the central part of what had been the village of Mure, where the Koreans suffered their exile. We 'chose' the spot for the Shrine 30 years before I received any of the above information. We were living and worshipping in a temporary space in Harajuku, Tokyo at the time. Odaisama's fame was spreading and there were always a lot of people coming and going in the house. I was in graduate school at the time, and quite frustrated that I didn't have a quiet place of my own in the house to study.

One spring I came to the Mitaka area to take a stroll in Inokashira Park. I passed a bamboo grove, with a grassy spot in the middle. I lay down for a rest in the grove and remember thinking how wonderful it would be to have a house in such a peaceful place.

That started the process that led to the eventual establishment of our home, Shrine, and research institute in this very place. The spot where I lay down in the grove is now where we have the sacred purification well at the entrance to the Shrine precincts. (Rinsing of the mouth and washing of the hands in such a well before entering a Shinto Shrine is a common ritual.)

After we purchased the land for the Shrine it was revealed to me that I had lived there in my first Japanese incarnation 3500 years ago, but now I learned that my family's karma to the place went much deeper. The Koreans we exiled to Mure were a proud and educated people; their sudden loss of wealth and power, coupled with their basic imprisonment on foreign soil, caused them great suffering. Many of the souls were not yet appeased; the karma was not resolved.

I was instructed to hold a memorial service for these souls on March 17th for five years. March 17th seems to have been the date that the ancient Koreans performed their annual ancestral ceremonies. I was also told that the resolution of the karma with the Korean souls would most likely aid in a shift towards better relations between Japan and Korea.

We held the ceremony each year from 1984 to 1988. While conducting the final ceremony, I could see an official-looking man beaming down on the proceedings. He was wearing an apron-like robe on top of a white silk garment, and had two topknots beside his ears. He indicated that he was very pleased, and I felt a great easing among the suffering spirits.

I don't know what connection there is, if any, but the relationship between Japan and Korea has been steadily improving. The South Korean Prime Minister made the first State visit here in many years. South Korea itself is enjoying new-found prosperity, and successfully hosted the Olympics in 1983.

Another interesting sidelight is that the city decided to dredge and clean Inokashira Pond for the first time in the park's history. It is as though purification on a spiritual level has the power to purify on the political and physical level as well. Though we speak of different kinds of karma, they are, in fact, all interwoven and interconnected.

Global Karma

The creation of an environment able to support life is a vastly complicated and awesome task. The earth, furthermore, appears to be the only planet in our solar system that can presently support life. How was this made possible?

According to geophysical and astronomic theory, the earth came into existence about six billion years ago. At that time the solar system was composed of interstellar gas, a portion of which began to cohere into a mass. Frequent explosions occurred within this mass, caused by nuclear fission and fusion. As a result, substances of light mass rose to the surface and those of heavier mass sank into the centre. The earth thus gradually evolved from a gaseous mass into a substantial one.

A hundred million or so years later, continents and oceans appeared. Organic matter was gradually generated in the sea. Proteins, microbes and amoebae came into being. The earth began to support an oxygen-based atmosphere similar to that of today. Single cell organisms aggregated into more complex beings, eventually evolving into the higher life forms of animals and plants. Ramapithecus, generally assumed to be the predecessor of man, was born about six million years ago. After undergoing various changes, Ramapithecus evolved into Homo Sapiens, the ancestor of present-day human beings, who first appeared on earth approximately one hundred thousand years ago.

According to modern physics, mass and matter are forms of packed energy, but physics has not explained whether or not matter has the ability to pack energy and give it form. From a non-physical perspective, however, it is clear that spirit precedes matter. Spirit creates matter, matter does not create spirit. In a series of experiments at the Institute for Religious Psychology, we have found evidence that strongly supports the notion that mental energy is capable of packing physical energy, transforming it into mass, and giving it form.

Planets that are able to support life are in the forefront of material, physical evolution. There are life-supporting planets in other galaxies, whereas planets like Mars and Venus are in pre-life stages. If we travelled as far out as Andromeda, we would find planets that used to support life systems similar to ours but that have since completed that stage.

All planets support spiritual dimensions, even if they don't support a physical life system. Spiritual and astral entities do not need a planet with trees because they can live without oxygen; they can exist in the midst of an inferno and not get burned.

Evolution

All things exist first in the spiritual dimension, then they gradually actualize in this dimension. This is evolution. The future of the material world, events that will happen millions and billions of years from now, already exist in the spiritual dimension, in the world of ideas.

According to the theory of evolution, complex life forms develop slowly in continuous sequence from the first, simplest, forms such as the amoeba. I do agree that evolution proceeds from the simplest to the more complex, but disagree that the process from lower to higher life forms is consecutive. It appears to me that the progression proceeds in evolutionary leaps, mutations if you will. I do not see a progressive evolutionary process from monkey to man, but, rather, a sudden leap in the process that distinguished one from the other. The original human form already existed in the spiritual worlds, and when the material world had undergone sufficient preparation and ape-man had created the right moment, evolution stepped in, took a leap, and human beings were born.

The evolutionary process may seem cohesive when viewed from a materialistic standpoint, but I am quite certain that it is not. At some point, each stage of evolution seems to cut off. I believe that Spirit lies behind the discontinuous succession of evolution, supporting and sustaining the process. The amoeba does not evolve into a human being. Spirit in the non-physical dimension creates the amoeba, giving it life, then goes on to create other forms. Spirit does this by creating a form suitable to its desired manifestation. It then enters into the form and a living, physical entity is born. Spirit and matter are distinct and separate entities.

Mind and body are likewise distinct entities. An evolutionary stage is determined by the degree that the mind is independent of and extends control over matter. In this light, humans have reached a high stage of evolution compared to other beings on the planet. Most other animals are capable only of spontaneous response and reactions to a given environmental stimulus in accordance with a limited amount of knowledge gained through past experience. The human mind has the capacities of imagination and abstract thought, though it is normally restricted by the limited information given to it by the physical senses. Yet the human mind has the capacity to transcend the limitation of the physical body and the outside environment. In the astral and causal dimensions the mind can function free from the dependence and limitations of the physical body and the physical universe.

A mind which has become even partially free from its material manifestation goes to a correspondingly non-physical realm upon death. The spirits of the dead form differing levels of society in the astral and causal dimensions according to their level of spiritual evolution. Though non-material, the astral and causal dimensions are still subject to karmic law. There are even higher dimensions that do exist. These are the celestial dimensions of Divine manifestation, and they are not regulated by karma. They act to control the primordial energy that pre-exists any phenomena of manifestation and are responsible for the creation of the physical universe.

The earth, then, is not only comprised of the physical planet but also of the astral and causal worlds that belong to it. Human beings, who are liberated to some degree from the power of matter, have been moving in and out of these dimensions for tens of thousands of years. Each stay in the physical realm tends to last 50 to 100 years, and tends to hundreds of years in the others. The intrinsic and instinctual drive towards spiritual evolution is the reason behind all these comings and goings.

On a planet that supports life like the earth, the spiritual dimensions and the physical dimension are intimately interwoven. On lifeless planets this is not the case; there is a great gulf between the spiritual and physical entities. On earth we live interconnected to all the elements that make up the earth's natural environment as well as with the Soul that exists behind them. Understanding this interconnectedness underscores the need for us to exist in harmonious balance with the natural environment and the other dimensions. When imbalance occurs, karma determines retaliation.

Nowadays we are seeing nature retaliating to her destruction by physical phenomena such as floods, famine, and earthquakes. On the human level, society still suffers from unending discord because of one tribe or nation asserting itself to the detriment of others. This is true not only on earth; there is disharmony between the societies of the astral dimension as well. Disharmony and imbalanced inter- action is a sign that the entire sphere is still at a halfway stage in its spiritual evolution.

Though peace will take time to achieve and many will suffer in the process, I see the earth evolving towards perfection rather than devolving into global holocaust. As humankind evolves it will increasingly free itself from mat- ter. This will enable it to attain a state of pure love and gain an essential control over matter. When humankind is able to fully control matter, it will gain eternal life and true spir- itual wisdom. There will then finally be a realization of the Kingdom of God here on earth under God's power. I feel that we should seek and prepare for the idea of a world religion at that time.

I foresee that this state of earthly heaven will continue for thousands or possibly millions of years. Then our universe, including the earth, will die, leaving only the world of pure consciousness and the celestial dimension behind. Every- thing will ultimately return to the Absolute.

CHAPTER FIVE

Towards a Theory of Karma

Through my experiential and experimental study of karma and reincarnation, I have concluded that these phenomena are governed by clearly defined principles. I believe they are regulated by natural law as rigorously as the more scientifically demonstrable phenomena of gravity and electromagnetism. Because the ability to directly perceive the non-physical dimensions is a prerequisite to a thorough understanding of karma, mystics rather than scientists have been our main sources of information on the subject for many centuries. The Upanishads and the Buddhist scriptures, for example, offer much discourse on and explanation of karma, some of which is helpful to modernday comprehension and some of which simply echoes the perceptions of others and isn't based on direct experience.

As humankind continues to evolve, I foresee the emergence of a unified theory of karma that will become scientifically accepted. I believe this knowledge will have a profound effect on morality, religion, on all aspects of human organization. I hope that the work I am doing in this lifetime will prove a contribution to this endeavour.

A viable theory of karma needs to address a number of basic issues. Are human beings really reborn? What happens at death and where do we go from here? How and where is karma stored? What conditions induce karma to manifest and lead a person to reincarnate?

Let me attempt to address each of these issues in turn, building on the material already presented.

Are Human Beings Really Reborn?

Hinduism and Buddhism unequivocally teach that reincarnation happens to everyone until their soul evolves to a state where it no longer needs to manifest on earth. My work in spiritual consultations certainly seems to verify this principle. Certain cases, such as that of Ms. Y., have even lent themselves to historical corroboration.

I notice that a growing number of clinical psychologists, particularly in the United States, are using past-life therapy in their practices. Celebrities are writing books about their past lives. There are quite a few parapsychologists now seriously documenting purported cases of reincarnation. One of the luminaries in the field is Dr Ian Stevenson, a professor at the University of Virginia Medical School. In 1966 he published a well-respected work entitled *Twenty Cases Suggestive of Reincarnation*. He has documented cases of reincarnation in many different cultures, and has found examples of alleged reincarnation in cultures as diverse as those of India, Turkey, Thailand, England, Canada, and the Inuit people of Alaska.

Dr Stevenson visited my Institute on his way home from conducting research in India and Thailand. He told me about one case I found particularly intriguing.

An Indian man had come to see him while there, a man of about fifty. He claimed to clearly remember one of his past lives. He said that he had been a British military officer at the time of the First World War. He was killed in battle when a bullet pierced his throat. This bit of information is interesting because the Indian man had twin birthmarks on either side of his throat which, Dr Stevenson noted, did look like bullet scars. Dr Stevenson showed me a photograph of the man and the marks were clearly visible.

The man proceeded to tell Dr Stevenson in detail the facts of his former life. He remembered the name of the town in Scotland he was from, peculiar words and expressions in the local dialect, the names of his parents and the location of his house. He described other identifying features of the landscape, and a hilltop outside town that contained the ruins of a church.

Dr Stevenson verified that the Indian man had never travelled to Scotland or England, and had no practical way of obtaining this information.

After a thorough interrogation, Dr Stevenson flew to Scotland to determine the authenticity of the man's story. As far as he was able to tell, everything the man described was true. The town does exist. Its appearance, down to its street names, are just as they were described to him by the Indian man. The words of the dialect are exactly as the man had spoken them, and there is a family by the name of the one he claimed to be his own.

Dr Stevenson's investigation convinced him that the British officer was reborn as the Indian man. He proved to his own satisfaction that there was no way in the world that the Indian man could have known as much as he did about the British officer, his small Scottish town and his family. This appears to be an authentic case of rebirth.

Some parapsychologists would disagree, attributing supposed cases of rebirth to clairvoyance and the ability to see into the past or the future. They would claim that the Indian man was clairvoyantly able to see the town in Scotland and that he gained his information by such means. In the case of Ms Y., the woman who I saw had been the daughter of Nakanose, a parapsychologist might claim that I was clairvoyantly able to see that Ms Y. was going to Suwa where she would enter a certain library and obtain certain information. Then, he might say, I gave her clues to reinforce the future activity. In this way, the parapsychologist could dispense with the incident without having to bring the subject of rebirth and the soul into discussion. He would remain rooted in a scientific discipline limited to materialistic understanding.

For individuals who have vision that functions in the nonphysical dimensions of reality, however, the knowledge of rebirth of the soul is inescapable. For the Indian man who knew that he had been British, rebirth is a fact, not an issue.

As increasing numbers of people begin to experience the fact that they have lived many lifetimes, I believe that awareness of reincarnation will enter the mainstream of human knowledge.

The Mechanism of Death

The great Indian saint Yajinavarga lived during the age of the Upanishads (800-500 BC). He was the first to encode a clear explanation of karma, transmigration, and death, which we find in the Upanishad entitled the Brhadaranyaka.

He explains the stages of death in the following manner, using the Sanskrit term Jiva to refer to the individual spirit in the causal dimension.

1. The individual being stops functioning in the physical dimension when the heart stops beating.
2. The astral body, which has completed the task of recording the results of the actions of this lifetime in the form of karmic 'seeds', moves to the heart of the physical body (the Anahata Chakra in the astral).
3. The Jiva enters the astral body and 'A light shines from the top of their heart.'
4. The Jiva slips out of the corpse 'through the eyes, or the top of the head, or some other section'. By this he means the Ajna Chakra, the Sahasrara Chakra, or some other Chakra.
5. When the Jiva leaves the body, the life force goes with it. The Veda states, 'The organs of consciousness follow the Jiva.' This means that both the mind working in conjunction with the physical body and that of the astral dimension leave the physical body with the Jiva. When the Jiva leaves the physical body, the energy and the organs of consciousness of the other levels go along with it.
6. 'The Jiva is now constrained by its knowledge and behaviour gained in former lives.' This means that the

Jiva's karma determines which spiritual realm the Jiva will go to and how it will live, and when it will be born again into this world.

Odaisama had a severe heart attack in 1966. She lay unconscious in Tokyo University Hospital. The doctors said they were not sure if she would live. I sat with her, holding her cold hands, praying continuously and sending her energy. After 24 hours she opened her eyes for the first time and was able to take a sip of water. When she had completely recovered, she described the experience to me: 'As I was lying there unconscious, I saw a beautiful golden light emerge from my heart and form itself into a shining twirling ball. The ball travelled through my shoulder, down the inner side of my arm, to the tip of my little finger, where it hung suspended. As I was watching it, I realized that if the ball separated from my finger I would die. I decided not to resist, to flow out of myself with the light. At the same moment I heard a voice saying, 'You must not go.' The ball of light suddenly returned up the path it had taken, re-entered my heart, and disappeared. At that moment I woke up and found you praying so earnestly beside me.'

You can imagine my surprise when years later I read the description in the Upanishad that so closely mirrored Odaisama's experience, but with two major differences.

The first obvious difference is that she did not die. The process of death was severed and she was able to continue to live. Because the Jiva did not enter the astral body entirely, she was able to observe the movement of the astral body.

The second important difference is that Odaisama's Jiva did not attempt to leave from the heart chakra itself, but travelled down the meridian pathway controlled by the heart chakra to the tip of the little finger. On the following page is an illustration of the heart meridian. As you can see, the pathways are identical.

In my case, when I leave my physical body during samadhi, I do so through the Sahasrara Chakra at the top of my head. When I heal people I send energy directly from my Ajna Chakra between the eyebrows or alternatively

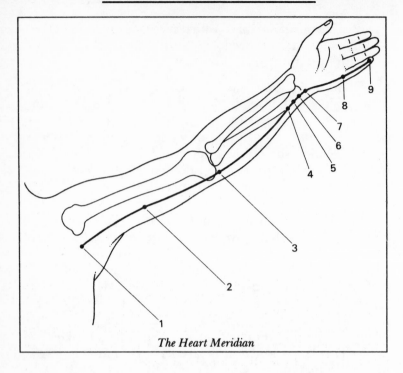

The Heart Meridian

project it from my palms or finger tips. But I didn't see the connection with death before.

Further years of observing the death process have shown me that the soul does indeed enter the astral body and then exits the corpse either directly from a specific chakra or from the end point of a meridian controlled by that chakra. The karmic make-up of the person determines which chakra/meridian complex he or she will exit from. This in turn influences where the soul will go after death.

People obviously accumulate karma on all levels of their being during a lifetime, but there is a dominant karmic aspect that has most generally formed the individual's character and behaviour. This is reflected in the level of their spiritual evolution and in the chakra most active at the time of death.

People generally leave their bodies in the following manner:

The soul and astral body of a person with karma of strong sexual and materialistic attachments moves from the heart to the Svadhishthana Chakra below the navel. The Svadhishthana Chakra controls the unconscious and the urogenital system through the Kidney and Urinary Bladder meridians. These pathways run down the legs and terminate at the tips of the little toe. The soul and astral body travel down the meridian and exit from one of these endpoints.

The soul stays in the astral body and is born into the lower realms of the astral world where it leads a life of suffering. As we have seen from previous examples, beings in this state are characterized by selfishness. Their attachment is so strong that they tend not to reincarnate for a long time.

The soul and astral body of a person with the karma of strong attachment to the emotions and imagination moves from the heart to the Manipura Chakra above the navel. The Manipura Chakra controls the emotions and the digestive system through the Stomach and Spleen meridians which also run down the legs. The soul and astral body exit through one of the endpoints in the toes.

These souls continue to inhabit the astral body. If they are unable to control their emotions or imagination through the agency of self-awareness, they are destined to suffer in the lower astral realms. The souls who are aware of their emotions and imagination and are capable of controlling them live enjoyable lives in the upper parts of the astral world. Actually, their lives there are not very different from those here on earth. Whether in the lower or higher astral realms, this category of soul reincarnates most frequently. They desire physical bodies to help them control their emotions and imagination, thereby enabling spiritual growth.

The spirit and astral body of a person who had devoted his or her life to the betterment of the world rather than to personal gain, who has attained an evolved state of love and compassion goes directly from the Anahata (Heart) Chakra down the Heart meridian, on the underside of the arm and exits from the tip of the little finger. The spirit goes directly to the causal dimension.

The soul of a person who has attained true wisdom and who has no more earthly attachments passes from the heart to the Ajna Chakra between the eyebrows and then to the Sahasrara Chakra at the top of the head where it exits directly into the causal dimension.

When a being goes directly to the causal dimension, its astral body also 'dies'. However, the seeds giving it the potential of future physical and astral manifestation are stored in the causal body.

The causal dimension is a paradise filled with love and intelligence. Residents there live long and healthy lives, free from the distinction between male and female. The atmosphere is charged with vitality. In this happy environment, the souls endeavour to further their spiritual growth.

When the spirits in the astral dimension have contact with those in the causal dimension, they perceive them as beings of light rather than as figures. Causal beings often act as guardian angels to individuals or communities they are related to in the astral and the physical dimension.

In the Bhagavad Gita it says, 'And he who at the end of his time leaves his body thinking of me (the Supreme Being), he in truth comes to my being: he in truth comes unto me. For on whomsoever one thinks at the last moment of life, unto him in truth he goes, through sympathy with his nature.' One's thoughts and ideas at the last moment of life play an important role in deciding where one will go and how one will next reincarnate.

About 40 years ago a widow came to Odaisama, asking for a spiritual consultation. She wanted to know how her mother and her husband were doing in the other dimension, because they had an illicit sexual relationship with each other while they were alive. When Odaisama meditated, she perceived that the husband had deeply repented his unfaithfulness at the last moment of his life, and that he was enjoying his life in the astral dimension. Her mother, on the other hand, was suffering from a guilty conscience about her daughter and simultaneous attachment to her lover. The widow asked why the mother was the only one suffering when they had both betrayed her.

Odaisama explained that her husband had experienced true repentance at death, and was able to place his faith totally in God. This enabled him to move to a place in the higher astral dimension where he was making a sincere attempt at spiritual growth. On the other hand, although the mother was convinced she had been immoral during her lifetime, she had no twinges of conscience about it during her death. Now she is suffering the karmic effects of her actions in the hell of the lower astral dimension and it will take her a long time to reincarnate. People like her husband, who admitted his mistakes and asked God's forgiveness, can reincarnate easily and often lead exemplary, righteous lives. They always have to protect themselves, however, from the inclination to repeat similar immoral actions in the next incarnation.

Karma: The Mechanism of Storage

We always think of reincarnation in terms of this world, of being reborn here, but the same thing can be said when we think of reincarnation from the side of the astral dimension. From that side, it feels like when one dies one has to go to the physical world and stay there until one can be born again into the astral dimension. It's the same thing as we feel about death, but from the opposite direction. The individual goes back and forth, back and forth, never once leaving a dimension of manifest karma.

What actually happens to the karma of all the actions performed over so many lifetimes? Are all actions recorded or just some of them? Where and how is karma stored? What causes karma to manifest in a certain way at a given time?

I began a formal search for the answers to these questions by studying the exant literature on the subject, but found that my experiential information generally superseded what I was able to discover in traditional theory.

One example of this is the question of recorded and unrecorded karma. Early Buddhist theologists believed that the results of actions are stored in a latent, or seed (Samskara) form. This, from my experience, is true. However, the theologians also asserted that not all actions are recorded, not all actions produce seed forms that will manifest at a later time. The Buddhists divided activity into two categories, unintentional and intentional. Unintentional activity is anything of a purely physical, habitual, or ritualized nature. Intentional activity is any movement that occurs as a result of personal judgement.

They based their reasoning on Shakyamuni Buddha's teachings about karma, in which he emphasized its moralistic aspects. He stressed the necessity of attaining the dimensions of reality that transcend good and evil. He taught that since the mind is what determines the goodness or evilness of an action, the mind itself is manifest karma. The theologians thus concluded that only self-determined activity could result in recorded karma. That is, only intentional actions can become seeds stored in the Causal Consciousness. They felt that since something like physical exercise has no relationship to good and bad and because it is nothing more than a physical movement it cannot produce an effect that will remain, i.e. be recorded.

I do not agree with this interpretation. Take the example of the Indian man discussed before whose neck had been pierced by a bullet. The piercing itself is neither good nor bad; it is just one form of physical movement. However, when the man was reincarnated in this life, he was born with a disfiguring birthmark on his neck where the wound had been. In this way, the karma of the physical piercing cannot be said to have been unrecorded.

About three years ago a man who was suffering from epileptic seizures came to me for a spiritual consultation. When I began to meditate, I saw a soldier fighting in the Second World War. He was a tank commander on a South

Pacific Island, and he ran into an American Army position. He was met with a hail of bazooka fire, and as he leapt from the vehicle clutching his sword, a bullet caught him in the stomach, killing him. I asked the man sitting before me to show me his abdomen, as I wondered whether the bullet wound of his former life would remain as a birthmark. When he showed me his abdomen, there on the left side was a black and blue birthmark about 2.5cm in diameter. I then told him what I had seen. He was quite amazed, because it turns out that he had an uncle who was a tank commander in the South Pacific who had been killed in the way I described. The man had never met his uncle, who was killed five years before he was born. But his whole life his family had told him how much he resembled his dead uncle in looks, personality and character.

I then psychically confirmed that indeed, the uncle had been reborn as the nephew. The uncle was quite a heroic figure. He was highly trained in the martial arts and sacrificed his life willingly for his country. He had no regrets about dying. In his desire to defeat the enemy, however, he continued to do battle in the astral dimension after his death. Even after he was reborn onto this earth, he continued to be deeply attached to this warrior self in the astral dimension. His astral consciousness was so strong, in fact, that it had the power to overwhelm and dominate his ordinary waking consciousness. This was the reason for the epileptic seizures he had been experiencing.

Again we have a case where a bullet wound in one lifetime has left a scar in another. The passing of a bullet through the flesh is a physical movement; in and of itself it is neither good nor bad nor intentional. Therefore, according to Buddhist theory, it should be unrecorded karma that should not be stored. If this were so, there would be no effect from one lifetime to the next. The birthmarks of the Indian man and the epileptic seem to disprove this theory.

The result of any action takes the form of latent energy patterns that we call a seed. I believe that these karmic seeds are stored in the chakras of the astral and causal dimension, according to their specific nature. I think that the abdominal birthmark of the former tank commander is the karmic result of seeds being stored both in the astral and causal dimension. The moment he was struck by the bullet he felt a burning sensation, and then a terrible pain. The emotional attachment he paid to the pain, his mind's emotional attachment to the pain, remained as an impression, a seed in a chakra of the astral dimension. Because the causal body is the most fundamental to human existence, the fruits of every physical action an individual performs are stored within it. I believe that the black birthmark on the left side of the man's abdomen was caused by a seed that was kept in the Svadhishthana Chakra of the causal dimension. This is because the Svadhishthana Chakra is responsible for the formation of the physical body. So when the foetus of the new being was developing in his mother's womb, the seed expressed itself in the formation of the birthmark. The emotional energy of the astral dimension enhanced the degree of manifestation of this particular karmic result.

Buddhist theory holds that all karmic seeds are stored in causal consciousness. It appears clear to me, however, that the seeds can be stored in the chakras of the astral body as well. The distinction appears to occur in the following manner:

When a person is emotionally attached to the result of an action, the ensuing karma is stored as a seed in the astral body. When a person is not emotionally attached to the result of an action, the karma is stored in the causal body. The karmic condition of each chakra is reflected in the associated meridian network that controls the circulation of Ki energy throughout the physical body.

What follows is a general outline of where different types of karma are stored in the astral body and which meridians are affected.

Muladhara and Svadhishthana Chakras

The seeds of sexual attachment, among the most powerful and troublesome for humankind, are kept in the Muladhara and the Svadhishthana Chakras of the astral body. These two chakras control the functioning of the urogenital system, sexual desire, and the unconscious. The associated meridians are the Kidney, Urinary Bladder, and the Small Intestine.

Manipura Chakra

The seeds of karma generated through attachment to the emotions and the imagination are stored in the Manipura Chakra. This chakra controls the functioning of the emotions, the imagination, and the digestive system. The associated meridians are the Stomach and the Spleen.

It is a common experience for many people that emotional stress causes stomach problems. From the meridian standpoint, it works both ways. Digestive dysfunction can also be said to produce emotional instability.

Ms Y. was a prime example of this. Her intense emotional attachment to romantic love was stored in the Manipura Chakra. When she reached the age at which the previous events had occurred, the seed manifested through her Manipura Chakra. She became very emotionally unstable and at the same time she developed various digestive problems. When we tested the functional state of her meridian system with the AMI (Apparatus for measuring the functioning of the Meridians and the corresponding Internal organs) we found severe abnormalities in the Stomach and Spleen meridians. This is a common pattern. We often find these abnormalities before either emotional instability or digestive disturbances actually occur. I have concluded that when a seed beings to manifest, it affects the corresponding chakra and meridian system before it manifests in the mind and the physical body.

Anahata Chakra

The seeds generated from attachment to love and compassion are stored in the Anahata Chakra, which controls the circulatory system and the power of love and compassion. It is related to the Heart and Heart Constrictor meridians.

Vishuddi Chakra

The Vishuddi Chakra holds the seeds generated from attachment to purification. This chakra maintains the existence of the physical entity through control of the respiration and the skin. Its associated meridians are the Lung and Heart Constrictor.

Ajna Chakra

The seeds of karma generated by attachment to knowledge and wisdom in the course of activities like scientific research and spiritual practice are kept in the Ajna Chakra, which controls the brain and thereby the body. This chakra is closely related to the Governor Vessel, Urinary Bladder and Small Intestine meridians.

As long as there is attachment to phenomena such as sexual desire, love, or knowledge, emotions and imagination accompany them. This emotional and imaginative content causes such karma to be stored in a chakra of the astral body.

When a human being acts intentionally or unintentionally without attachment to the results of the action, the ensuing karma is stored in the causal body, in so far as he or she holds on to the self as distinct from others.

Physical characteristics and habitual gestures also fall into this category. This becomes quickly evident when dealing with astral beings who often bear a great resemblance to who they were on earth, down to such details as the way they smile.

Many astral beings continue after death to make the same characteristic gestures as they did when they were alive as human beings. Sometimes I ask a surviving relation in a spiritual consultation if they know anyone who often gestures in a certain way, and the person will answer with something like, 'Why, yes, that was a habit of my dead mother's.' When astral beings speak, they often maintain characteristic intonations that can help identify who they are. When the individual is reborn again in this dimension, they bring with them the potentiality of similar habits and gestures. I have come to believe that, whether in this world or the next, all actions, no matter how insignificant, are recorded and stored in the causal body and have the potential to manifest at some future date.

Karma: Mechanism of Manifestation

Once karma has been stored in the seed state, it lies latent until conditions arise that cause it to manifest. My work led me to formulate a number of general hypotheses about how the manifestation of karma occurs.

Manifest karma is that which is actively functioning in any dimension at any given time, that is, the manifestation of the results of a former action (usually sustained activity or behaviour). On the physical plane, actions that produced strong attachment in a past life become the generating factors for the present incarnation. The results of these past deeds manifest and are active in this lifetime. The karma is no longer latent as seeds in the chakras of either the astral or causal body. In Ms Y.'s case, the actual experience of the results of the attachment and sorrow which she experienced in her previous life manifests as depression and emotional instability. When karma manifests in this world, when it is functioning, it is in the process of being fulfilled.

The fulfilment of karma brings the opportunity for one to dissolve it. If one attaches to the results of the present circumstance and tries to suppress its expression, the karma will continue. But if one simply lives out the manifestation without attachment, while making one's best efforts for others for society in whatever position one finds oneself in, the manifest karma will eventually dissolve and be gone. To cite a previous metaphor, it's like opening a bottle of soda. At first there is a lot of carbonation, but after a few minutes the fizz decreases and finally disappears. If one is alarmed at the explosiveness of the fizz and tries to put the cap back on the bottle, it is like forcing the karma which is on its way to dissolution through manifestation back into its original latent condition. Such repression means one will continue to experience the results of the karma for more lifetimes instead of just getting rid of it.

Karma which is open is informative:
karma which is latent is not

I sometimes come across cases where the karma of the person does not reveal itself easily. When someone's spirit is involved in a specifically strong karmic circumstance and is not free, then the karma isn't always easy for me to see. For example, some years ago, a Mr T., who had practised yoga and meditation very diligently for a number of years, moved to a new home. Nearby there was a large mound, which was an old tomb. On the day he moved he developed a high fever, and began vomiting. He went into a rapid decline and those around him were very afraid for him. They prayed together and called on me for help. I went to the Shrine to pray. In a number of hours we were able to stabilize Mr T.'s condition.

While I was praying in the Shrine, the resident spirit of the old tomb appeared before me. He had a face like a Noh theatre mask and was wearing ancient-looking white robes. He stared hard at me and disappeared. This happened two or three times, but he gave me no information. For several days after this I myself was sick, bedridden with fever. I knew I had encountered an extremely negative and power-ful spirit.

When Mr T. came to thank me and later when he came to the Shrine to meditate and pray, I tried to discover who the spirit was, when he had lived, and what he had done. With the assistance of the Higher Being during Samadhi, the answers to these questions finally became clear. About 1000 years ago, this man was sent from the capital of Nara to Musashi, where his tomb is located. His position was that of the imperial official in charge of horsebreeding, an extremely influential position at that time. He was accused of taking bribes and expanding his own influence with this money, and he was severely punished by the government. The man died bearing a potent rage against the government. He has lived in the astral world holding this grudge for 1000 years. During this time he has developed certain occult powers and has become able to exert a strong influence on others. He has gained the power to conceal his identity, to block its revelation to others.

Generally speaking, the karma of spirits who are bound by deep-seated resentment or terror as the result of their deeds and who have lived in the astral dimension for a long time without reincarnating is not easily revealed. The spirits resent attempts to understand their karma and will do what they can to stop the process. When one tries to force them into revealing their karma, various misfortunes or accidents can result from the spirit's resistance, determined by the extent of their power. In contrast, karma resulting from non-attached action is generally open and informative. When I enter samadhi I can easily see the details of the causal relationships involved in such a being's karma.

When the knowledge of a certain karma is open and accessible to me, it tends to manifest within an individual's lifetime, or at the latest, in the next incarnation. The degree that the karma will influence the individual, the group, or the environment involved depends on the degree of the karma's fundamental relationship to the existence of same.

*Examples of when karma might manifest in this lifetime,
in the next lifetime, or be suppressed for a long time*

A woman desires to enter a good university, so she studies
very hard. After a couple of experiences of failure, she
finally passes the entrance exam. A man wants a promotion
at work and makes great efforts to that end. His effort is
recognized and he gets a promotion. These are simple
examples of how the results of deeds in this life manifest in
this lifetime.

Efforts made in this lifetime can combine with similar
efforts made in previous lifetimes to produce very beneficial results. This is often the case with spiritual awakening.
When a person devotes him or herself to a spiritual discipline and attains the enlightenment to teach and guide
others in their spiritual search, it is usually the result of
many lifetimes directed towards this aim.

The birth of a baby is another common result of combined karma from the past and present life. The birth is the
result of the sexual union of the parents and the strong
personal relationship that the baby has with one or both of
the parents from a previous lifetime.

The actions that you are most attached to in one lifetime
usually become the cause of the next manifestation. Ms Y.
and the tank commander are examples of this.

In Ms Y.'s last lifetime the action of love was what most
concerned and interested her. Her attachment was so great
that it took her 400 years to come back to this world. The
tank commander, on the other hand, reincarnated a mere
several years after his death. He had no attachment to
personal emotion, even though he was involved in a life and
death struggle that he continued beyond his death. His
action was done for the benefit of a nation, and transcended
personal benefit. He was therefore able to reincarnate
quickly as a citizen of the same country he had died for. It
should be noted, however, that viewed from a global perspective, the idea of one nation benefiting over another just
shows the selfish character of national karma and is not to
be commended.

A person reincarnates many times, in some cases hundreds of times. In some lives the individual is born as a woman and in some a man; in some lives he or she is born in the East and in others the West. A person creates a great deal of karma over their lifetimes.

What is most significant for a person at any given time is the most significant karma operating at the moment. But all actions are recorded, so we carry with us many less significant karma seeds that manifest continually under the rubric of the dominant themes. These lesser seeds may stay in a latent state for a long time, because they are suppressed in the astral or causal dimension by the energy contained in the more influential karmic seeds. When they are provided with sufficient energy to manifest, they will finally do so.

The karmic seed with the strongest energy
has the highest priority for manifestation

A seed stored in the astral or causal dimension is composed of the energy of that dimension. The stronger the attachment inherent in the seed, the greater the amount of energy it possesses. The seeds with the most energy have the highest priority for manifestation, and generally determine the character of the resulting individual.

The result of activities such as those done to gain knowledge about the truth of the universe or to somehow better mankind are stored in the causal dimension. The resulting individual of such dominant karma tends to be highly intelligent, intuitive, and often psychic.

When the dominant karma is from the astral dimension with a Manipura orientation, the resulting individual tends to be very emotional, but controlled, and has an active imagination. This describes a lot of people here on earth. When the dominant karma is from the astral dimension with a Svadhishthana orientation, the resulting individual tends to be materialistic, selfish, and has trouble controlling his or her emotions. Unfortunately there are a lot of people like that here too.

Astral energy is much more powerful than physical energy. The more astral energy in a given seed, therefore, the higher its priority for manifestation. The degree of astral energy in a seed is determined by the degree of emotional and mental attention given to the results of that particular action. When this degree is one of severe intensity, the process is reversed. Such intense attachment locks the seed into a cohesive state from which it is difficult to manifest.

When the karmic seeds in both the astral and causal dimensions possess strong energy, the interaction of family karma, geographic karma, social karma, and national karma etc. determines the priority of manifestation. In general, though, the causal seeds are from a higher dimension than those of the astral, their energy is stronger in quality and quantity, and so they have a priority for manifestation.

At the same time that dominant karmic seeds manifest to determine overall life structure, many thousands of seeds with lesser energy manifest and disappear one after the other throughout a lifetime. The results of these seeds may affect a person for days, months, or years, depending on their intensity.

*Techniques or knowledge mastered in one life
are likely to manifest in the next life*

From an early age certain people exhibit natural and conspicuous talents in fields such as music or mathematics. I sometimes come across the chance to see into such a person's previous lives, and find that they have made advanced studies into those specific areas before.

The seeds of knowledge or techniques mastered in a previous life are stored in a chakra of the astral or causal body, and are likely to manifest as an individual's talents or knowledge this time around. Subjects which haven't been mastered in a previous life are more difficult to master in this one.

The same can be said of spiritual practice. Those who have done yoga, zazen, or led a life of prayer as monks or spiritual practitioners in a previous life are likely to be attracted to such religious practice and devote themselves to such activities, and they tend to make rapid spiritual progress. Compared to these people, those who haven't done such activities make slower progress in this life.

Manifestation of the results of karma differs according to the individual's character

In the case where a usually righteous person unexpectedly commits a crime due to unusual circumstances such as adversity or drunkenness, the fruit of the action usually manifests during this lifetime, and the karma is done with. But when a habitually vicious person who has often caused trouble to others commits the same crime as the righteous man, the fruit of the action would become a powerfully negative seed as a result of the accumulation of other similar actions. The seed would manifest in a life of torment in the astral dimension and probably continue into the next incarnation.

This mechanism represents a kind of karmic safeguard. The result of the identical action will manifest very differently depending on the nature of the person who commits it. I believe that this is a part of the universal principle to discourage vice and encourage virtue.

Reincarnation

Expectant parents often ask me to select a name for their child. They sometimes do this at the beginning of the pregnancy, which really gives me a headache because even if I can communicate with the spirit of the foetus I still don't know definitely if it's a boy or a girl. Just because it has a male soul doesn't mean it won't be born female this time around and vice-versa. Also, at this point the soul is not always in the foetus but sometimes hovering around it, directing its growth.

Sometimes the spirit of the foetus starts to talk to me. It will tell me who it was in its previous life and what karmic relationships caused it to choose these parents in this one. The causal and astral minds and bodies of the spirit define its physical formation. The spirit first decided on its parents, either in accordance with the inevitability of karma or by its own free will. These parents are the ones who are karmically suitable to itself in character, constitution, and capability. It then decides on which genes to accept from the moment of union between the sperm and ovum, absorbs nutrients from the mother's body, and forms its own body. As the foetus grows, it creates the condition of its internal organs and corresponding characteristics in accordance with his or her karma. To again note commonly seen patterns, souls who have strongly sexual and materialistic karma will create a characteristic Svadhishthana Chakra and urogenital system that will manifest in their coming lifetime as difficulty in controlling their sexual drives and the functions of their unconscious minds. People with strongly emotional and imaginative karma will likewise create a characteristic Manipura Chakra with its corresponding functions in controlling the emotions and the appetite.

Individuals usually reincarnate through a combination of personal desire and the interaction of attendant manifest karmas such as those of the family and the group. But sometimes personal desire is enough to do it.

Examples I see where personal desire dictates reincarnation are a desire to marry the same person as before; to continue research in a certain field; to lead a comfortable, well-off life; to be a wise and just political leader; to be a religious leader. In such cases, the attachment to such personal desire is the overriding cause of the incarnation and the other karmas are not as relevant. The reincarnation is a show of personal power.

Most people reincarnate, however, after the complex interaction of personal karma, family karma, group and racial karma, environmental karma, and national karma have established the proper conditions for the manifestation of the individual. There are many spirits who desperately want to be born on the earth, but who are unable to realize their desire because of the complexity of establishing the correct environment.

Some people reincarnate very quickly. Something I see quite often in spiritual consultation is a person who formerly led a rather decent life concerning his or her work, family, and community, but who somewhere made a big mistake; usually to do, again, with sex, money, or power. These people die with a deep sense of regret for their mistake and an earnest desire to make up for it in their next life. Such an individual can often reincarnate in a few short years, even months, after his or her death. Children who die young also tend to reincarnate quickly, as do young soldiers who sacrifice themselves for their nation or their tribe. The motivating factor for reincarnation in the above cases is personal desire, aided by the other karmic factors; except for the case of a soldier, in which national or tribal karma becomes more dominant than the personal.

Sometimes people take an abnormally long time to reincarnate. As we have seen, this is particularly true when a being is exceptionally attached to the emotions and the imagination. Two cases already introduced are those of the protector divinity of our Shrine and the ancient government official in charge of horsebreeding. These two have both been in the astral dimension now for over a thousand years, one attached to happiness and one attached to resentment. Both have gained a certain degree of psychic power and are able to influence those around them, in both the astral and physical dimensions. The protector's influence is positive and harmonious while the official's is negative and divisive.

People who die accidental, tragic deaths have a difficult time reincarnating if they hang onto the pain and terror they experienced. We have cited numerous cases of soldiers stuck in this agonized state, and have stated that they can be helped by prayer and offerings to aid in their realization that they are dead so that they can move on.

I recently had a particularly difficult case. The spirit involved had been a soldier who nearly died of starvation while hiding from the enemy alone in a trench. The enemy found him and burned him to death with a flamethrower. The combined agony of starvation and incineration were just too much for this poor soul. We were able to help him release into the higher astral dimension, but it will be a long, long time before he reincarnates here.

Geographic, national and global karma can make reincarnation in a specific place difficult or impossible. It is difficult, for example, to reincarnate in an area that has been repeatedly used as a battlefield. This is because when a physical space is spiritually polluted it can be too uncomfortable to live there.

Thousands of years ago in the Sahara, nomads could live in grassland areas where the northernmost limits of the equatorial west wind brought occasional rain. Now, however, these northern limits have moved further south and no more rain comes to this area. It has become a desert. It is not possible for human beings to reincarnate into such a place. This impossibility is an attribute of geographic and national karma.

Suppose that the sun gradually cools, or that the sun becomes hotter and explodes into pieces. There would be no more solar energy reaching the earth and consequently the environment able to support life would be destroyed. Although the astral and causal dimensions would still remain, it would be impossible for human beings to reincarnate on the physical plane. Astronomy speaks of such possibilities for the future destiny of the earth and the sun. This is an attribute of global karma. When this happens, those who have not yet evolved out of the physical sphere will have to continue their quest for spiritual evolution without the advantages of the physical dimension.

A person is usually born into a cultural and physical environment very similar to the one he or she lived in the last time. In this sense it is true that we are products of our culture. This is the reason that Japanese are usually reborn Japanese, Europeans are reborn within Europe, Africans are reborn Africans, and Indians are reborn Indians. The karmic ties of race, nation, and geography all conspire to make this so.

Individuals inevitably act as part of a group, and the tie to a group can pull one to incarnate. Our Ms Y. is an example of this. She reincarnated into a situation where the people who had been her mother, father and lover in her previous life had already been reborn and were actually related as family through the attraction of group karma.

I often see that each action in certain personal relationships cumulatively adds to the group karma, which later leads to similar relationships in the next life. An individual reincarnates in order to make spiritual progress by fulfilling his or her karma in relation to the group karma that has been determined over the course of many lives. There are also cases of negative group karma where an individual's inclusion in it acts to impede spiritual growth. Therefore, once we have close relations with people, who are always karmically determined, we should try to have a good relationship with them based on love and wisdom.

I have noticed an interesting difference in general between the influence of group and family karma on Asians and Europeans. In Asia, people historically have been primarily engaged in agriculture. Asians settled into lands that were very lush, thanks to the abundant rain. They formed village communities consisting of their families and relatives; after death Asians tend to live in communities of their kin in the astral dimension and then to reincarnate into the same family here on earth. Their parallel lifestyle in the two dimensions exerts a crucial influence in deciding when and where they will reincarnate.

With Europeans, however, I often find that more importance is attached to an individual's chosen community than to his or her family unit. European souls tend to live with the spirits of their families for a short time after death, but later they live in a community of like-minded individuals. Their reincarnation reflects the karma of their community more than that of their family. Communities are also connected throughout the dimensions. If a community in the astral world is strong and exerts a powerful influence over an individual to stay there, it is difficult for that being to reincarnate here.

In summary, then, an individual usually remains in the astral dimension for a period of tens to hundreds of years, though some people reincarnate more quickly or slowly, depending on circumstances.

What about the spirits living in the causal dimension? How and when do they reincarnate?

Basically, these karmically freer spirits have the power to reincarnate at will. They also have the choice to remain in the causal dimension for a very long time, living existences filled with the highest level of love and wisdom. A soul in the causal dimension might be motivated to reincarnate on earth for some altruistic reason which will better human kind such as the desire to guide others towards enlightenment, to establish a new scientific or artistic truth, or to govern a large nation. When such a spirit decides to reincarnate, it selects the parents and circumstances most suitable for what it wishes to accomplish.

Beyond the causal dimension is the dimension of divinity, (Purusha in Sanskrit) which transcends individual karma altogether. If a being from this dimension desires to descend to earth in a messianic capacity, this of course would be an act of free will rather than a result of karmic conditioning. It would not be a case of reincarnation but rather the birth of a child of God.

CHAPTER SIX

Transcending Karma

Attachment to the self creates karma. Non-attachment to the self dissolves karma. How do we attain this non-attachment? Non-attachment to the self is made possible through the realization that the ultimate nature of the self is Empty; the self does not exist as a separate entity. A full actualization of this realization needs to occur; mere conceptual understanding does not lead to liberation. Many methods have been devised to help human beings attain this realization. These methods usually fall into two general categories, one we may call 'non-attached behaviour' and the other that of 'spiritual practice'. Through diligent application of these methods, an individual can free him or herself from the confines of a karmically determined existence. Enlightenment is real and attainable.

Chosaku

By relating karmic anecdotes I have been trying to demonstrate that all dimensions of existence are interdependent, those that we can perceive as well as those we can not. Nothing that is manifest exists by itself; an individual existence is possible only through its inherent connection to everything else. The fact that we manifest in bodies gives rise to the deluded notion that we exist as a separate self. We cherish this 'self'; we want 'it' to be happy and healthy and to live a satisfying life. This 'self' wants to get ahead in the world, even if it may be at the expense of others. It wants to live forever. It is ignorant of its true nature.

This ignorance is often referred to as 'spiritual darkness'. The first step in awakening from the darkness, again, is to realize that the independent self does not exist; it is not eternal; it is going to die. Once we can view the 'self' objectively, one can begin to take the steps necessary to liberate oneself from the domination of karmic law.

A theoretical and conceptual understanding of the nature of self is not enough to accomplish this liberation. A human being performs actions with a physical body and a mind that over lifetimes creates a backlog of karma. All this karma must be dissolved through present and future action before the human being can be free of it. At the same time, the person needs to act in a way that will not produce any future karma as a result of these necessary present and future actions.

The Buddhist term for the type of behaviour that does not produce karma is Chosaku. It is a difficult word to translate into one word of English. It means an action performed without consideration or attachment to the results of the action. It is sometimes translated as transcendental action or non-attached action, both of which seem awkward. In any event, Chosaku is an extremely difficult thing to achieve.

Performing an action creates a result. We usually perform an action intentionally for the result that we expect it will produce. The 'self' desires the result of the action. This desire creates attachment to the result of the action. This attachment creates karma. Because we believe that the 'self' exists, we believe that our 'self' is the main agent in any action we undertake. This belief is 'self' perpetuating and reinforcing. As 'self' based behaviour continues over time, as actions made by the 'self' accumulate, the tight karmic shell that surrounds the 'self' is made even stronger, giving an illusion of ever-increasing identity, separateness, and independence to the individual.

Whenever a person performs an action for its result, the 'self' is necessarily present and acting. The 'self' is the generating cause of the result, the karma.

The alternative is to perform an action without the 'self' as the generating cause, by discarding, negating the 'self' as the action is being performed. When the 'self' is absent, a higher dimension of one's being automatically manifests through the individual. This higher consciousness acts on the principle that the true good for any individual is the good for all. When the 'self' is not acting, there is no desire or attachment to the results of the action and therefore *the action does not create karma*.

This is the essential key to dissolving and transcending karma. Formerly created karma ensures that a person will meet with a continuation of events to which he or she will have to react. When an individual attains a state where they simply act to the best of their ability without attachment to the results of any given action, they are able to dissolve the manifesting karma rather than create more. Eventually their personal karma will disappear: they will transcend karmic limitations and unite with the higher levels of existence.

As a human being gains the ability to deny and negate the existence of the self, he or she automatically merges with increasingly high levels of being that express themselves in the actions that the body is performing. Through perfection of Chosaku a person attains the ultimate realization that all action is actually a manifestation of the grace of God, of the Absolute. The being realizes that God is beyond karmic limitations and is the complete support and nurturance of all living things. God is the governing principle of the universe. When Chosaku is fully attained, the body becomes the vehicle for the expression of the higher principle, the Absolute. The results of such behaviour, no matter whether they appear to be positive or negative, are determined by the will of the Absolute. By definition the results of such behaviour promote the harmony of the whole: they benefit the world and the universe as well as the individual.

At Tamamitsu Shrine our main scripture is entitled 'Tama no Hikari'. The original text from which the script was taken lay dormant for several hundred years in the head temple of the Ji-sect of Buddhism, Fujisawa Shojokoji. The original is a 20 volume work written in classical Chinese. Following the instructions of Lord Tamamitsu, we went and obtained the text from the temple. We chose certain important sections from the text as directed and translated them from classical Chinese into Japanese, thus producing the 'Tama no Hikari' scripture.

There are ten precepts within the scripture. They are:

1. God is the ruler of the myriad spirits.
2. When there is no Self, the voice of the Divine can be heard.
3. Your life and character are gifts from your noble ancestors.
4. Purify the old transgressions which run through your family.
5. Do not be consumed by sorrow or stricken with worry.
6. In the human world nothing is perfect.
7. When marital harmony is achieved, success in all things follows.
8. Apply yourself to your appointed task without seeking reward.
9. Your position is established by your actions.
10. Idleness summons all manner of demons and evil spirits.

Numbers two and eight bear directly on what we are discussing.

'Apply yourself to your appointed task without seeking reward.' Appointed task here simply means the duty inherent in any given situation. When a man joins a company, his task is to work for the company. When he marries, he incurs duty towards the woman as her husband. When they give birth to a child, he gains duty as a father. It is also his duty to react responsibly to whatever life beings him, to help someone he encounters who is ill or in trouble, for example. Obligation does not disappear when you, say, retire from your job. There are always things that you must do. The most important thing that you must do at the moment is your present task. We tend to confuse this issue because of our busy minds, but it is actually quite simple.

Apply yourself fully to your appointed task. This becomes a matter not of one's self acting, but becomes the process of the best being done. This precept counsels one to openly accept things as they are and not be attached to whatever outcome occurs. It teaches us to abandon both the self that is doing the acting and the self that is desirous of results, pointing the way to freedom.

When an individual becomes free, he or she can literally, intuitively, merge with the reality of another person and realize the feelings and conditions of the other's circumstance. He or she is able to act from a position of true wisdom rather than self-interest. As long as one is looking at everything with only one's own best interests in mind, the wisdom available to him or her does not reach beyond the limited framework of the self. This 'wisdom' is very narrow in scope. However, when one abandons the self and simply becomes the activity itself, the self which acts (the subject) and the object of the action become one. Subject and object become unified. The resulting consciousness, which transcends both the subjective and objective viewpoints, is a higher consciousness that gives rise to and encompasses both viewpoints.

It does not matter what the task is that needs to be undertaken, how 'trifling' or how 'important'. Whether sweeping the garden, or straightening out the shoes in the entranceway, the world operates by people doing the things that must be attended to at any given moment. No matter how boring you think a task is, things that must be done should be done. The reason a task is boring to you is because you are looking at things from the standpoint of worldly attachment. From the standpoint of the Absolute, all action is the same.

Chosaku is sometimes understood to mean the act of leaving the everyday world of the household to enter a monastery. This is misleading because it is naive to think that by entering monkhood someone automatically cuts all karmic ties to the outside world and flies into the waiting arms of Buddha. There is still much work to be done. In Burma and Thailand every young man is required to abandon the world and undertake Buddhist spiritual practice for a certain period of time. But putting on yellow robes in no way assumes that a person has attained the ability to perform Chosaku. Many people who take the external form of monks and nuns continue to commit self-serving acts.

The monastic tradition, however, is founded on very valid principles, because most people do require some form of sustained spiritual practice to help them transcend the self. Throughout the centuries, religions have developed countless methods to hasten and guide spiritual growth. I believe that the psychophysiological process of spiritual evolution that the human being undergoes is a universal one; the human interpretation of the process is what varies so greatly over space and time. One characterization of the process that I find uniquely clear and comprehensive is the one proposed thousands of years ago by the Indian Saint Patanjali in the Yoga Sutras. These sutras were compiled sometime between the second century BC and the fifth century AD.

The Yogic Process

Hindu yoga is much more than the physical exercises of hatha yoga generally associated with it in the West; it is a carefully devised system of spiritual development. The Indo-Aryans have been preoccupied with trying to understand the nature and development of consciousness for millennia. Two thousand years ago, when Patanjali was born, there already existed in India a multitude of sects and teachings based on the experience of countless mystics and yogis. Patanjali's major contribution was to cull the basic facts of the psychophysiological process of transformation

116

from all this information and to codify these into eight stages. He managed to discard a great deal of secondary information and subjective interpretation surrounding the process, producing a description that is concise and surprisingly free of dogma. These stages are generally represented in some form in any system of spiritual development, whether Buddhist, Christian, Taoist, Shintoist, Kabbalist, Shamanistic, or whatever.

As codified by Patanjali, the eight stages are:

1. Rules of abstention (*Yama*)
2. Moral precepts (*Niyama*)
3. Physical postures and exercises (*Asana*)
4. Regulation of respiration (*Pranayama*)
5. Introspection (*Pratyahara*)
6. Concentration (*Dharana*)
7. Meditation (*Dhyana*)
8. Union (*Samadhi*)

Yama and Niyama

The first two stages, abstention and precepts, teach self-control; they help one begin to disentangle oneself from the domination of egocentric desires. The two function together to help the seeker gain control of negative thought and action. Both are found in some form in all religious systems, just as the Ten Commandments form the basis of the Judeo-Christian ethic: Thou shalt and thou shalt not.

From a karmic viewpoint, the attempt to refrain from destructive actions and to lead a good life is the logical way to live. Because of karma you are inherently responsible for all of your actions. A negative act does not simply disappear; it gives rise to eventual repercussions through the law of cause and effect.

Though true in daily life, this becomes extremely important for someone who is attempting to go beyond ordinary human limitations. Without a basic level of self-control and stability it is difficult to maintain the degree of effort required for the awakening of other states of awareness.

Because such awakening brings with it higher forms of perception and power, self-centred misuse of the greater perception and power bears proportionally graver karmic consequence. Because such perception and power are those of a higher authority, it is dangerous to think that they are your own to use in your self-interest. Spiritual awakening brings with it the need for moral impeccability.

Asana

The third stage of Patanjali's description, asana, consists of the physical postures and exercises that we normally think of as yoga. Often these postures are maintained for an extended period of time. When the body is concentrated into a single position, the mind can be turned to the field of consciousness. Another important aspect of these postures is that they function to maintain a straight spine and to balance the flow of ki throughout the body.

The two postures used most widely for meditation in the East are the full and half lotus. If done correctly, these postures allow one to hold the spinal column as straight as possible, to release all unnecessary tension from the neck, shoulder, lower back, and arms, and to maintain – without strain – the centre of gravity in a spot about two inches below the navel.

Psychologically, anxiety locked in the body in the form of physical tension is a waste of energy and distracts from one's concentration. The meditation postures help to release tension. Muscle tensions in the lotus posture have been found to be lower than in any other body position except that of lying down. When all the organs of the body are in their proper places and no effort is needed to support them, nerve impulses and the circulatory systems of the blood and ki can flow freely. And once active consciousness is freed from having to control any physical processes, deep relaxation is possible. All the other yoga asanas are also designed to promote purifying circulation in the body by releasing energy blockages in specific places.

Pranayama

As the body is stilled through the practice of holding one set posture for a long time, so the breath is quieted through the practice of regulation. A yoga teaching states that if the mind is moving, so are the heart and respiration. When we are angry or excited, our breath quickens; when we sleep, our breath slows down. By consciously slowing down the breath and making it rhythmic so that consciousness is not disturbed by it, we can achieve a corresponding tranquillity.

One typical method of pranayama is to inhale slowly to a count of four, hold the breath in the area of the abdomen for a count of sixteen, and exhale to a count of four. This method, like the majority of the many types of pranayama, teaches one to breathe from the abdomen. Abdominal breathing calms both body and mind, and helps the mind to turn inwards onto itself. Pranayama also increases the amount of ki taken into and stored in the physical body. Along with the asanas, it improves the circulation of ki throughout the meridians. This helps to purify and balance both the body and mind of the physical and astral dimensions. Increased ki is needed for the intense concentration central to the meditative process.

Many different systems use breath regulation as a technique to alter consciousness. The Taoists, for example, teach a method called tenporin, or circulation of light. The disciple concentrates either on drawing the breath slowly from the coccyx to the head and back to the coccyx (the shoshuten, or 'lesser circle') or from the soles of the feet to the head and back down again (the daishuten, or 'greater circle'). Various Christian meditators also mention an equivalent of pranayama practice. For example, in *Method of Holy Prayer and Attention*, Simeon, the New Theologian (circa 1250 AD) instructs the monk: 'Then seat yourself in a quiet cell, apart in a corner, and apply yourself to doing as I shall say. Close the door, raise your mind above any vain or transitory object. Then, pressing your beard upon your chest direct the eye of the body and with it all your mind upon the centre of your belly – that is, upon your navel, –

compress the inspiration of air passing through the nose so that you do not breathe easily, and mentally examine the interior of your entrails in search of the place of the heart, where all the powers of the soul delight to linger.' Pressing the chin into the chest is a common yogic device to aid in the retention of breath.

Pratyahara

The Indian tradition often likens sensory intellect to a wild monkey. Just as the animal swings in a frenzy from tree to tree, screaming and chattering, the ordinary mind frantically attends to the inrush of sensory stimuli from the outside and the uprush of memories, emotions, and fantasies from the unconscious. An important step in the attempt to realize other levels of consciousness is to integrate this fragmented awareness.

In regard to the stilling of the mind necessary for the growth of awareness, Meister Eckhart said: 'The soul, with all its powers, has divided and scattered itself in outward things, each according to its functions: the power of sight in the eye, the power of hearing in the ear, the power of taste in the tongue. And thus they are less able to work inwardly, for every power which is divided is imperfect. So the soul, if she would work inwardly, must call home all her powers and collect them from all divided things to one inward work.'

The ways devised to 'call home the soul's powers' vary from system to system, but all require placing oneself in an environment and a psychophysiological state that make one less vulnerable to the intrusion of sensory stimuli. Mystics have traditionally isolated themselves as much as possible from the mundane world by retreating into caves and monasteries, by journeying to mountaintops and deserts. But such extreme measures are not necessary. Any clean quite space where one can sit undisturbed will do.

Withdrawing the senses in introspection automatically helps to suspend the activity of ordinary consciousness. Many effects of sensory withdrawal can be detected and measured physiologically. For example, one of the common pratyahara techniques is to close the eyes. EEGs indicate a significant change in the brain's activity even when the eyes are simply opened then closed. Alpha waves appear more frequently when the eyes are closed; beta waves appear as soon as the eyes are opened. Alpha waves correspond to a quiet mental state, beta to mental activity. Simple light stimulation will also effect many changes in the mind and body. A change caused by the stimulation of the retina by light sends electrical impulses to the occipital area of the brain, which governs visual perception. The impulses race on to the memory centre in the temporal lobe, then on to the frontal lobes, where the categories are stored that enable us to distinguish, for example, whether a colour is red or blue. Next, the brain relays nerve impulses to the body, causing many subtle and complex reactions, such as an increase in the secretion of glycogen (a substance produced in the liver which is necessary for muscle movement). In short, when light comes into the eyes, the brain and the whole body begin to respond automatically. Thus, by allowing in less light and keeping the source of stimulation constant, one can temporarily deactivate the functioning of the stimulation/response mechanism.

The mind, which was lost somewhere in the outside world, is regained. Now the work of real concentration may begin.

Dharana

Although the existence of the individual unconscious was not formally postulated by Western thinkers until the mid-nineteenth century, it has been clearly acknowledged by the philosophical and spiritual traditions of the East for thousands of years. The experience of the Eastern thinkers taught them long ago that ordinary, sensory-dependent mind has two parts – one we are actively aware of and one that we are not. The individual unconscious is the storehouse of all egoistic desires – 'egoistic' in the sense that desires are a product of the illusion that self exists separate from other.

Not only did the Eastern (specifically Hindu and Buddhist) traditions recognize the existence of the individual unconscious, they also realized its enormous complexity, depth, and power – its power to influence our thoughts and actions in a way that maintains the illusion of self as distinct from other, thereby preventing unification with nonsensory states. The individual unconscious is the greatest obstacle one must overcome in breaking through the sensorily created shell that limits us from participating more directly in reality. The tools of concentration and meditation are employed to overcome this obstacle, to undermine the control that the individual unconscious and its attendant karma exerts over us.

Concentration is the act of riveting attention on one fixed source of stimulation. Patanjali defines it as 'fixation of thought on a single point.' The point chosen is the object that the meditator is attempting to unify with. It might be any number of things depending on the type of practices. I usually counsel a specific chakra or a specific manifestation of the Absolute (a certain Deity, perhaps.)

The mind and body normally exhibit varying degrees of activity, depending on the amount and type of stimuli being received, but the activity is continual. This activity prevents unconscious elements from taking over the field of awareness, though they are free to enter. When one chooses a single point of concentration and holds onto it, awareness is forced to stop running around.

Directing all one's attention to one point produces a temporary simplification of the operations of the brain and corresponding sensory consciousness. Awareness is thereby released from its ordinary occupation, that of attending to a multitude of stimuli. Because this task acts as a barrier to the direct intrusion of the unconscious, once the field of awareness becomes quiet, the energy-packed contents of the unconscious spontaneously begin to spill over into the other territory. We see this happen whenever the normal function of awareness is suspended, when someone is drunk or hypnotized for example.

The factor that enables one to become conscious of the unconscious is often referred to as 'the observer' or 'witness consciousness': it is the ability to watch the flow coming out of the individual unconscious without becoming involved in the drama – the ability to disassociate oneself. The observer is a spontaneous product of the practice of concentration and the meditator is admonished repeatedly to strengthen the observer by paying attention to the object of concentration and letting go of whatever comes into his or her mind. The observer becomes increasingly able to watch silently as various contents stream through the quieted field of awareness.

In the beginning stages of any concentration practice, the observer has not yet gained the power to withstand the deluge coming from the unconscious. It soon disappears as the field of awareness is overrun with memories, thoughts, feelings. When meditators remember their task, they again begin to direct attention to the object of concentration, letting the subconscious contents go right past them, paying no attention to them. This process is continually repeated, until the concentration span can be controlled.

As the subconscious contents continue to be released, they lose their repressed energy. A state is reached in which ideas and memories rarely drift into the field of awareness. Then the mind becomes truly quiet. Such total silence can only be maintained for very short periods at first (a second or two) but the duration lengthens with practice. This silence is accompanied by a feeling of deep peace and indicates that the practitioner has entered the initial stage of meditation, a spontaneous psychic continuation of concentration requiring no new technique. A common physiological manifestation of this stage is that the respiration rate, normally 16 breaths per minute, will automatically decrease, usually to around 10, but sometimes as low as 2 or 3. Saint Theresa called it the 'Orison of Quiet' and places it, in the exact same manner as Patanjali, after 'Recollection' (voluntary concentration) and before the 'Orison of Union' (samadhi).

We noted that Patanjali defined meditation as 'a current of unified thought'. A later commentator, Vyasa, enlarges this definition slightly, saying that meditation is a 'continuum of mental effort to assimilate the object of meditation, free from any other effort to assimilate other objects.' The attainment of the stage of meditation brings with it a change in the subject's relationship to the object, and a merging of the two begins to take place.

In the early stages of concentration it is difficult to become one with the object because of the disruption of thoughts and emotions. Through repeated practice, one gradually achieves unification with the object for brief periods of time as the thoughts and emotions dwindle. Becoming one with the object in the astral dimension, even briefly, is a negation of the physical self that stands in opposition to the astral object. This constitutes the completion of the stage of concentration.

In the following stages of meditation, the self is negated and identification with the object is deepened for increased periods of time that stretch for 2 to 3 minutes. At this point contact may begin to take place with beings of the astral dimension. Spiritual possession can occur at this stage, and may need to be dealt with. This is one reason why it is advisable to meditate with a qualified teacher. Other evidence that this stage has been reached is that extra sensory perception of events on the physical and astral dimension begins to manifest.

The first seven stages of the yogic process purify first the physical mind/body and then the astral mind/body. Physical desire, such as that for food and sex, become controllable. One is free in the sense that you exert control over desire, it no longer controls you. Another physical effect of this purification is that the physical senses become exceptionally sharp. As the astral self becomes purified, one gains control over the emotions and the imagination. One gradually gains control over certain non-sensory modes of perception and behaviour ('psychic powers') such as ESP and psycho-kinetic ability. As one gains control over these abilities, one loses attachment to them, just as one has with the physical senses.

Samadhi

Consciousness, now concentrated and still, attempts through continual active awareness to communicate directly with the object. At this stage of meditation, the realization occurs that the object can be cognized directly, without the aid of the senses and mental categories, but there is still a lingering sense of the 'I', or separation between subject and object. It is as if the shell surrounding the individual, the shell of the self, has become punctured with holes, and through these holes the subject is able to merge with the object and experience it directly. The longer this state is maintained, the larger these holes become, until the shell eventually dissolves and total unification takes place between subjective consciousness and the other. One cannot complete this process through one's own power, but needs to rely on higher sources. (I will discuss this in the next section, *Surrender*.)

Patanjali enumerates a number of gradations of samadhi, which are all states of union but in which subtle illusions of self as distinct from other are still maintained. The final state is called asamprajnata samadhi, of which Mircea Eliade says: 'The Yogin who attains to this samadhi realizes the dream that has obsessed the human spirit from the beginning of history – to coincide with the All, to recover Unity, to re-establish the initial non-duality, to abolish time and creation (i.e. the multiplicity and heterogeneity of the cosmos), in particular, to abolish the twofold division of the real into object/subject.'

Attaining unification, even partially, with an object of the causal dimension means that self-negation and identity with the object on the astral dimension is achieved and complete. As one continues through practice to purify the causal self,

self-negation in the causal dimension takes place leading to a final liberation into the dimension of Pure Consciousness that exists beyond the realm of karma. This is the ultimate attainment of the human being.

From a karmic perspective, the soul is freed in the following manner. Before the causal mind/body has begun to be purified, the effects of actions done in the physical and astral dimensions are stored as seeds in the chakras of the causal mind/body. These karmic seeds unremittingly manifest and extinguish in one's lives on the physical and astral planes. As the causal mind/body begins to be purified, however, a significant change takes place. The energy of the stored seeds can be dissolved directly through Chosaku and the yogic process before they ever manifest. This greatly facilitates the dissolution of karma because if a seed does not manifest it cannot cause the creation of further karma for the individual. Eventually, all the seeds that could manifest as the karmic bonds that result in reincarnation are dissolved and there is no longer the need to manifest as an individual human being. The soul has reached a certain enlightenment and is free to move into the Divine Realm of Pure Consciousness, no longer bound by karmic restriction.

Surrender

Learning yogic techniques, standing on your head, controlling the breath, meditating – all these things will make you physically healthier and may cure certain emotional disturbances. But in so far as these actions are being performed by the deluded self they are rooted in attachment and worldly desire. To undertake a practice for the purpose of transcending attachment and the dissolution of karma is to practise in the true sense of the word. Even while one is meditating, if one continually holds onto the self that is doing the concentration, one cannot expect to attain spiritual progress or evolution. The need to consciously practise

Chosaku applies equally to everyday life and to spiritual practice.

An individual can only go so far in the yogic process by his or her own power. A person who has purified the physical and astral planes is like a glass that had once been filled with dirty water and is now filled with pure water, or a glass that was once full of water but is now empty. The glass itself still exists. The shell surrounding the self, though brittle, still exists.

It is impossible to break through this shell of the self by one's own power. One must rely on the greater power of the higher dimensions to effect the total breakthrough. To do this requires the recognition of and total surrender to the higher power, the proverbial leap of faith. When one surrenders, one receives the power from above to break through the limiting shell. This is a dialectical process that is repeated many times throughout the process of spiritual evolution.

Because people so cherish the self, surrendering it is a very frightening experience. A person may experience the surrender as a leap into an abyss or as death. This is because he or she has not yet attained a complete trust and faith in God, the complete assurance that once the self is abandoned, the being automatically merges with a higher stage of existence which is necessarily ready and waiting to accept it. This is universal law; there is no capriciousness about it, no chance for the process not to function. Diving into God is more like diving into the ocean. The water is all around you and it supports you as you float blissfully relaxed. At the instant of surrender, the entire being of the individual merges into the specific higher manifestation of reality that it is in relation to at that point in its development.

This surrender, this going from reliance on one's own power to dependence on the other, is often experienced as a state of prayer. True prayer, not the profit-seeking kind where we ask for the solution to problems. In true prayer, the self praying to God is forgotten and one becomes the prayer itself. God streams into the prayer and into the soul that has managed to negate the self.

Mantras are prayers that function in this manner. Each mantra is a linkage to a certain aspect of the absolute, a certain manifestation of Divinity. In true mantra practice, one forgets the fact that the self is chanting, becomes the mantra itself, and attains a state where nothing but the mantra exists. One's being then connects with the higher being the mantra represents. Many Japanese belong to the Pure Land sect of Buddhism which is dedicated to Amida Buddha. They practise a mantra called the Nembutsu. When a practitioner is able to abandon the self and attain the true Nembutsu, he or she experiences immeasurable light streaming into his or her being from Amida Buddha. A real connection has occurred.

The Absolute in its goodness gave these means to human beings for their liberation: Chosaku, spiritual discipline, the mechanism of surrender, and prayer. I encourage you to practise them.

CONCLUSION

I believe that when the physical, astral and causal dimensions reach a balanced state, this world will disappear. I imagine that this is going to take a few billion years. All the karmic dimensions, both the physical and the non-physical, are born, develop, and when their purpose has been achieved, disintegrate into the original Absolute. As part of this process our universe was born, our sun came into being, and the earth began to exist. The ultimate aim of conscious spiritual evolution is to hasten the universal process by which we as a race attain reunification with the Creator of the Universe. I wish you blessings in your efforts towards enlightenment.

AFTERWORD

Since compiling the main body of this text, I have been studying the problem of the evolution of the world's religions and of religion's relationship to science. Much of this work has been published in Japanese, and will be coming out in English as *The Unification of Religion and Science*.

There are a few ideas about this subject that I would like to briefly note here, as they fall within the scope of our discussion on karma and reincarnation.

As we look back on the history of mankind, we see a progression in the degree of influence that the various types of karma came to exert over the individual. When people lived in small, largely unrelated communities, personal, family, and natural karma were dominant. As group ties proliferated, tribal and geographic karma began functioning. As the world's population grew and began to settle in large communities and cities, racial and territorial karma became increasingly operational. Mass warfare began. As feudal states emerged and grew into the present system of the modern nation state, national karma began to increase its influence over the individual. National karma is presently very strong, and warfare continues.

From an economic, communications, and environmental standpoint, it is clear that the world is poised to move beyond the nation state system into a more efficient, integrated global system. From a karmic standpoint, this means that global karma is gradually becoming more active. Examples of this trend abound: the ever-growing interdependency in the world economic and ecosystems; the increasingly unified satellite and fibre optic information transmission systems; the rising global concern over the pollution of the earth's oceans and atmosphere and the depletion of the ozone layer.

International politics are presently based on the theory that a balance of power among nations is a key ingredient for world security and prosperity. This theory isn't working. There are right now real conflicts occurring all over the place: the Sunni-Shiite split in Islam, the Israeli-Palestinian problem, and apartheid in South Africa, to name but a few examples. Such conflicts are rooted in religious, racial, and territorial disputes where the corresponding karma continues to exert a great deal of control over the individuals involved. The earth grows enough food to feed itself, but each day 26,000 children die of starvation because food is not distributed to them for largely political reasons. There is obviously something very wrong here.

As global karma becomes more dominant, I believe that the nations of the world will evolve beyond this outdated notion of a balance of power to a political position of true cooperation and harmony. I have foreseen that this utopian state will occur in about 250 years, but I have also seen that the earth will continue to endure much suffering and conflict before this next stage is realized. Psychically, the possibility of nuclear war continues to exist even though it no longer appears to me to be a definite eventuality, as it did a number of years ago.

As we move politically and culturally towards a world federation, a more globally oriented religio-philosophical system will also evolve. I believe, in fact, that an evolutionary leap will occur in what we call 'religion' itself, because I believe that the traditional religions are too grounded in regional karma to provide the universal tools necessary for a mass spiritual awakening.

I have made a study of this regionalism issue. Religious historians often discuss the differences between religions propagated in the desert, i.e. the West, and those of the forest, i.e. the East. There are aspects of this discussion that are pertinent to my notion that no existing religion can evolve per se into a universal one.

The original distinction between the two categories of religion is based on humankind's essential dependence on water. We have retained the ancient water of the oceans in our body fluids. The nutrients we take into ourselves are dissolved in these fluids and delivered to the cells that thrive on them. Sixty to seventy per cent of our bodies are composed of fluid; a person weighing 150 pounds contains approximately 90 to 110 pounds of water. On the average, we excrete 2.5 quarts of water daily by various means, and this must be replenished.

Desert regions contain little water. Searching for and obtaining water was the ultimate priority for the early desert tribes. Their lifestyle and ideology began from this search. In these areas, people were actually aware of the colour of the sand, the smell of the wind, the humidity, the types of shrubs and how they grew, and other geographical features. They used this information to judge where water might be found. Once a decision was made as to the location of water, the desert people would head in that direction without hesitation.

In an environment where there can be no alternative judgement, the separation between the self and the other, mind and object, man and God, naturally develops. This can be formulated as the logical proposition that A is A but not B. Two fundamental characteristics of the religions originating in the desert, such as Judaism, Christianity, and Islam, are that there is a demarcation between man and God and that man can never become God.

In contrast, the religions that originated in the water-rich lands of Southeast Asia, Buddhism for example, teach that man can become Buddha. In Hinduism, Taoism, and Shintoism, racial heroes and ancestors were worshipped as gods. Man can become God.

In those regions, abundant rain falls at regular and specific times of the year, the trees have luxuriant foliage, there is much fruit and food. People live on and farm land that has been graced with the blessing of rain. They experience the external life force of nature and the universe, with which they live in harmony. People are raised and nurtured within this life force, and recognize the workings of God through the continual manifestation of this abundant nature. Everything is essentially God.

In contrast to the logic postulated earlier, the logic of the forest religions can be formulated as A is A and A is B and A is C. Everything exists in a state of non-dualistic harmony beyond confrontation. Another way to express this formulation is A is not A nor B nor C. This underlies the Mahayana Buddhist assertion, first postulated by Nagarjuna in the second century AD, that the essence of existence is Sunya, or Void. Subject and object cannot be differentiated, so there is No-Thing.

The religions of the desert and those of the forest characterize the Absolute in terms consistent with their ideologies. Desert religions conceptualize an Almighty God who possesses human qualities and who is seen as the Creator of the Universe. Much Judeo-Christian thought concerns the reconciliation of the coexistence of such human and omnipotent qualities.

Living alone in an environment as harsh as that of the desert entails great difficulty, and people naturally banded together in tribal communities. For the community to function properly, rules had to be established, the most fundamental of which are the Ten Commandments. Those who broke the rules were severely punished by patriarchal authority.

The early patriarchs were charismatic figures who assumed full responsibility for the well-being of the community. They were single-heartedly devoted to the nurturance and support of their people. In return, the members were deeply devoted to their leader. Through this mutual respect and support the community was able to maintain cohesiveness and stability. In such a 'give and take' social structure, people conceived of God as an extension of the patriarch; He was a human-like God who possessed the perfect attributes of Absolute Authority and Absolute Love.

It is speculated that the notion of God as the Creator is again linked to the rain analogy. There is a parched desolate desert, a desert with little trace of life. Suddenly rain falls, revivifying the land and those who live there. God is seen as the generating force that enables life, hence the Creator. God created all things and rules over his Creation.

A corollary to the theory that God created the universe is that a beginning and an end to it exist. Christianity teaches that the universe will eventually come to an end and that all people are destined to be subjected to an ultimate Judgement Day. If one leads a moral life and believes in God (or Jesus Christ as Saviour), one will be admitted entrance to Heaven. These guiding principles have served to unify and stabilize Christian communities throughout the ages.

The forest religions, with their differing ideology, characterize the Ultimate principle as the Absolute Void that transcends all existence. The Absolute Void, or Nothingness, manifests itself into all existence, including a Deistic pantheon. Existence is seen as ceaselessly changing. Throughout the seasonal cycles of nature, flowers bloom, trees bear fruit, and leaves fall in a never-ending cycle. For these religions, nature and life reincarnate eternally. They do not postulate an end to the universe. In contrast, the religions developed in the desert regions believe that an individual's life is a one-time event – they deny metempsychosis (migration of souls). The religions developed in the forest regions believe that man and all living things in the universe reincarnate time and again, that life is an eternal process.

Variations in human behaviour and circumstance are also accounted for differently in the two types of ideology. Actually, the notion of evil and inequality has proven to be quite problematic for the desert religions. God, being omniscient and omnipotent, represents the perfection of Truth, Goodness, and Beauty. The patriarch, in his wisdom, reflects the attributes of the Creator. His actions, as well as all human action, are seen to be essentially creative acts that are made possible through the support of the omniscient and omnipotent God.

This raises many questions. What is the causative reason behind an act of free will? If we are created equally in God's image, how do we account for inequalities in ability, environment, physique, wealth, social position? Basically, how can people created by the God of perfect Goodness commit evil?

In the religions that developed in the forest, these questions are answered, as we have seen repeatedly throughout this text, by the theories of karma and reincarnation, functions governed by the Absolute Void. An individual is responsible for his or her actions, and the results of these actions determine the individual's present and future circumstances. What we term evil is any act that attempts to preserve the self to the detriment of the other. Acts of Goodness promote harmony within the Absolute, acts of evil, division. Karmic theory affords an explanation for the differences and inequalities among us.

Historically, another major difference between the regional ideologies is how they view the relationship between mind and matter, between the spiritual and the physical. The religions of the desert teach that in the beginning God created Heaven and Earth and then created the human body in His image. He then breathed life, or spirit, into the human body to create the human being. So from the beginning, mind and matter were seen to be distinct and in a dualistic relationship. Nature was there to be conquered. This subject/object dichotomy, which is presently being challenged by particle physics, has led to the tremendous development of the natural sciences, which has been of central importance to the material evolution of the race. But this dichotomy has also led to an increasing split between spirit and nature, between science and religion, and this has been its own source of anguish in the modern age. It appears that there is presently a need to learn from the non-dualistic, transcendent philosophies of the forests. Some form of synthesis is in order.

I believe that the evolution of a globally-oriented religio-philosophical system will be supported both by scientific enquiry and by transcendent spiritual principles. It seems to me that such a system will need to incorporate four basic suppositions.

1. The Absolute is Void. It transcends and is free from all existence. Thus it can create the universe.
2. Karma and reincarnation are the organizing principles of existence.
3. The non-physical underlies the physical; religion underlies science.
4. Human liberation is to reunify with the Absolute. Man can become God.

This crucial reunification with the Absolute requires the fundamental understanding that such unification is indeed possible: that a human being can become God. It further depends upon the recognition that the Absolute is Void, that It transcends and encompasses any individual manifestation of God that the human spirit can experience. The coming system is therefore inherently non-exclusive. The teachings of present-day religions will come to be recognized as valid but non-universal expressions of the Absolute as encountered in a specific time and place by the religion's founder and his or her followers.

I expect that the forthcoming system of spiritual evolution will accept karma and reincarnation as fact, and that its proponents will continue to explore the details of how these phenomena effect existence. I also think that scientific research will increasingly verify the unified nature of existence, and in so doing will objectify the principles of reality in a way that will render them more readily acceptable to our materialistically oriented world. As science increasingly recognizes the non-physical basis of physical reality, the age-old split between 'scientific' knowledge (subject/object dichotomy) and spiritual knowledge (subject/object unity) will at long last heal.

APPENDIX A

Questions about Karma and Reincarnation

The following questions are frequently asked when I lecture on karma, so I thought it might be useful to deal with them in a question/answer format.

1. *One of Buddhism's basic theories is that because of the impermanent nature of existence, there is no Self, no Ego. This appears to contradict karmic theory which postulates the existence of an individual self that runs through past, present and future and which creates its mode of existence through individual actions. How do you reconcile these two theories?*

Shakyamuni Buddha taught both the theory of No-Self and that of karma, but never explained how the two were related. The debates over this issue raged on for hundreds of years until the arrival of Nagarjuna. He was finally able to quell the dispute by elucidating the existence of the causal level of consciousness. This is the key that enables the reconciliation of the two positions.

No matter how stridently a Buddhist theoretician declares that 'There is No Self, No Self!', the fact of the matter is that each one of us obviously has something that we call the self. We have an 'ego'. And the fact that we cling so stubbornly to this 'self' is what causes us to transmigrate for many generations.

People are ordinarily so immersed in the world of karma that they are unable to see karma itself. But from the perspective of higher consciousness we can see that a given individual was at one time a man, one time a woman, one time good, and one time bad, through the process of many lifetimes. In this sense it is true that the non-permanent self that does exist in the karmic dimension has as its basis an unchanging Self, which we have been referring to as the Causal Body/Mind.

To reiterate, the Causal Body/Mind is the soul that we have originally received from God. It resembles the glowing orb of the sun. The Buddhists call it the Alaya Mind/Body, the Hindus call it the Jiva. It is Adam before he sinned. The causal entity differs from the Absolute in that it has been individuated and has entered into the karmic dimensions. Although it is individuated, however, it does not have its own nature, for it is wholly supported as an existence by the eternal Absolute. Essentially it has 'No-Self'. Until one becomes enlightened, abandons the Self, and extinguishes one's being within God's, one is trapped in the cycle of birth and death. Enlightenment ultimately means returning from where one came, to God. To accomplish this, one must eventually deny and transcend the Causal Self. The Causal Self appears permanent from the standpoint of the karmic world, but ultimately it, too, must extinguish itself in the Absolute. When extinguished, it becomes Absolute Nothingness and Absolute No-Self. This is how we resolve the seeming contradiction between the facts of No-Self and karmic reality.

2. *If all phenomena are impermanent, doesn't this mean that all phenomena instantaneously disintegrate? How is continuity established?*

The word karma comes from the root Kri, a verb that means to act. Karma means that a certain deed or action becomes one cause that produces a certain result. The result itself becomes a cause and one more result is produced, in a repetitive chain. For this to occur, there must be a universal principle which underlies both the cause and effect. If each time the phenomenon occurred it extinguished completely, the law of cause and effect could not have come into being.

However, it is clearly stated in Buddhism that all phenomena are impermanent. What this really means is that all existence, all phenomena, all activity is ceaselessly changing. Nothing remains in the same form for even an instant. If a human being is born he will assuredly die; the earth itself will some day disappear. Taking a more microscopic view, we know that the countless cells of our bodies are continuously being born and dying. The vital functions of our hearts and respiratory systems are constantly in a state of change. If we pursue this line of reasoning, where does it take us?

I am now here talking to you. At first I face right and talk, then turn to the left. You watch me as I face to the right and then to the left. If we pursue the view that 'all phenomena are impermanent', certain Buddhists would say that the me who is turned to the right talking and the me who is turned to the left are different entities. In other words, the me who was facing to the right was extinguished in an instant, and another similar entity arose when I turned to the left. The thing that existed here for a moment is extinguished, and a separate thing is born. Since a similar something appeared, in this line of reasoning, you would conclude that the two are not the same thing, that 'A' does not continue as 'A', but continues as a set of distinct entities 'B', 'C', 'D', 'E'.

When we push the idea that 'all things are impermanent' to the extreme, we arrive at the theory of 'instantaneous disintegration'. There is something quite strange about this notion. Even though we can recognize the aspect of sameness, this theory postulates that nothing remains the same for even an instant. Yet there must be something that forces us to recognize the aspect of sameness. The fact that we can say that phenomena are always changing suggests that there exists something in the background that does not change. We can link this to the relationship of a clock face and the hands that move around it. We can recognize the movement of the hands because of the existence of the stationary face. If the entire entity changed, we would not be able to recognize the transformation.

If it were true that everything was extinguished and recreated moment by moment, instant by instant, there would be no unifying principle continuously active throughout them. The ideas of karma and cause and effect assume that there is something between the cause and its results that links them together. And we find that, through the experience gained in spiritual awakening, there most definitely is a process in which each individual soul undergoes transmigration in accordance with the actions (the causes) of former existences. It therefore appears to me that the one-sided views of the 'impermanence of existence' and 'instantaneous disintegration' are not fully informed; they neither help us understand the problem of karma nor do they correspond to the facts of reality.

3. *What is the difference between karma and fate? If everything is karmically determined, I don't see the point of making any effort to achieve anything.*

This question recently came up in a spiritual consultation. Here is the reply the consultee was given.

'If you were very hungry, wouldn't you desire something to eat?'

'Of course.'

'Now let's say I place some delicious food on a high shelf. Are you going to sit there and wait for the food to fall off the shelf, or are you going to stand up and reach for it?'

What would any of you do in this situation? Naturally you would stand up, raise your arm up to the shelf, and grab the food. This is karmic action. If you decided that the food might fall of its own accord, you could just sit in front of the shelf with your mouth open and wait. Unless the shelf breaks, you could sit there for one hundred years. You would starve to death in the meantime. This is acting out of a belief in fate. Human beings must act to be able to eat. One of our ten precepts is 'Actions determine status'. This means that one's station in life, the boundaries of one's existence, are determined by one's actions. Nothing is begun if nothing is done.

Action is necessary to life. The notion of fate is antithetical to an understanding of karma in that it is an abandoning of action. Fate is a lazy belief – one in which you decided that the universe is moving in a certain fixed direction that has been ordained by God, and that you will allow Him to move you along in the same direction. Sometimes things will be good and sometimes they will be bad. There is no reason to do anything. The state brought on by these attitudes is more like being asleep than like being truly alive. It is like being a grain of sand swept along in the current of a great river.

If you have no priorities, if you wait for the food to fall, the value and meaning of your life will disappear. Human-like behaviour will not be generated, such as that which tries to better the world, better oneself, and affirm the existence of the individual. If you believe in fate you will not be able to find the meaning of your individual existence.

4. *It is often said that when we die, a parent or our grandfather or somebody comes to meet us. Is it true that there are loved ones waiting for us on the other side?*

Assuming that the relative or whomever has not yet been reborn and still exists in the spiritual dimension, and that you have an intimate karmic connection to them, it is very possible that they might come to pick you up. But you may not always be so happy to see the person who is waiting for you.

Here is something from my own experience. My maternal grandmother's family name was Yoshima. This family line was begun by someone who was related to the Heike Clan and who fled to the island of Yoshima in the Inland Sea about 800 years ago. The family lived there until the beginning of the Meiji Era (1868) when they moved to Shodoshima, where I was born. A few miles away from Yoshima is an island called Onigashima which was home to a gang of pirates for many years, when piracy was rampant in the Inland Sea. I'm not sure which side of the law the Yoshimas were on, but I do know that there was a tremendous amount of bloodshed throughout the family history.

About 35 years ago I began to see a recurring scene from this history: a bloody battle between two villages, and a frightening female ghost who had either been killed in the battle or who had committed murder herself. When my grandmother was dying, my mother went to take care of her, but I had to stay in Tokyo. I kept having powerful visions of this ghost – I would suddenly get into a state where I was physically unable to move my body but in which my consciousness was wide awake and very clear – and then I would see this woman. When my mother came back to Tokyo after my grandmother's death, she kept talking about how just before my grandmother died she kept saying over and over that she was seeing this awful woman, and she described her in minute detail. It was the same woman that I had been seeing at the same time but in a completely different place. My grandmother, by the way, was not a psychic and was not used to such experiences, but at the time of death she was able to see into another dimension.

In this case, my grandmother was not a woman of strong faith but her family karma was so strong that this woman was coming to meet her. My grandmother, because of her connection to the ghost, had a very rough time of it when she passed into the realm of the dead. This karma was strong enough to enable the spirit to come to meet my grandmother, but it was not positive karma. To believe that the beings coming to pick you up on the other side are only beings that you want to meet is very naive.

5. *Do we recognize who it is that's coming to meet us?*

Yes, you do. Even if you don't believe in things like spirits, when your consciousness weakens at the time of death, you begin to see various things. This is true when you die a natural death – it is not true if, say, you commit suicide by overdosing on drugs.

6. *I have a number of questions about Causal Consciousness. First, is it true that one can't have a mystical experience without going into Causal Consciousness?*

Yes, this is true because the dimension of Causal Consciousness is the only dimension in which it is possible to make a direct connection with the Absolute, and thus to have genuine mystical experiences. In the astral dimension it is possible to have psychic experiences like simple clairvoyance or ESP; they are of a lower and different nature from true mystical experiences.

7. *When one has mystical experiences in the Causal Dimension, do karmic seeds still exist?*

Yes.

8. *You know how we normally forget things that have happened to us in the past, but when the opportunity presents itself we suddenly remember them. Are karmic seeds like that?*

Memories from this life are stored and can be recalled from Causal Consciousness. When the memories are necessary or when circumstances jog them they come into consciousness. This process works fairly easily, just as when you address a computer. However, memories from past lives are a different matter. In most people the circuit connecting the present body and Causal Consciousness is not really functioning. In rare cases, the circuit connecting the Causal Consciousness through the astral mind and the subliminal consciousness to waking consciousness is functioning and these people can narrate the stories of their past lives.

9. *During spiritual consultations you often speak of certain karma that is presently manifesting. However, isn't it true that besides presently manifesting karma there is a lot of karma manifesting that we simply are not conscious of?*

Of course. One example is that when you become completely exhausted and lose normal self control, you may experience unusual shifts in your ordinary moods, ways of thinking and behaviour. In this case, karma outside that which is mainly manifesting in you comes strongly into play. There is much karma that unconsciously influences our behaviour.

10. *I don't understand how Chosaku can be characterized as non-desirous action. It seems to me that, being alive, human* *beings must necessarily possess a certain degree of volitional consciousness. Therefore, isn't it true that when you determine to become closer to the Absolute or to perform Chosaku you are, in a sense, exercising your will and desiring a result?*

This question shows that you are attached to only one condition of Chosaku, that of not desiring specific results of your actions. What we really mean by this is that you shouldn't desire results that are beneficial to you, the individual, because the point of Chosaku is to move into a level of consciousness that is higher than individual consciousness. The aim of Chosaku is spiritual evolution. Ultimately, however, one moves into the Absolute where the notion of result does not exist: within the Absolute there is No-Action, No-Cause, and No-Result. Chosaku can bring you into this world and, in this sense, Chosaku does have an aim. This aim is to transcend the realm of individual karma.

11. *Various books detail different ways to actualize the purpose of existence. For example, some suggest that by constantly holding an image of the actualized state in your mind you can naturally attain it. What do you think of methods that attempt wish-fulfilment through input into the subconscious?*

Methods of psycho-cybernetics and visualization are popular self-help tools. It seems to me that you can achieve some degree of success with them, but basically they are methods based in desirous action. They utilize the powers of the individual unconscious and of the imagination, which, by definition, limit their effectiveness to the individual realm.

12. *When we reincarnate, does all of our being reincarnate or does part of our being naturally disintegrate in the process?*

No results of desirous activity naturally disintegrate. Instead, they follow the law of cause and effect, and repeat over and over again. This situation continues as long as the manifest realms, both the physical and the spiritual, continue to exist. And, I believe, when the manifest realms are extinguished the seeds of desirous activity remain with God. When a new universe comes into being, the seeds sprout and the whole process begins again.

13. *Can Causal Consciousness be extinguished as long as the universe exists?*

The universe consists not only of the physical world but of the non-physical realms as well. When all of these realms disintegrate the Causal dimension will naturally disappear. This will take many billions of years. Can you wait that long?

Editor's Note:

Regrettably, Dr Motoyama is unable to offer spiritual consultations to readers. Due to demand, these are now available only to a limited number of Tamamitsu Shrine members in Tokyo. It is Dr Motoyama's earnest wish that the information in this book will help readers to understand their own karma and to know how to dissolve it more effectively themselves.

APPENDIX B

Other books by Dr Hiroshi Motoyama

How to Measure and Diagnose the Functions of the Meridians and Corresponding Internal Organs, Institute for Religious Psychology, Tokyo, 1975
Hypnosis and Religious Superconsciousness, Institute for Religious Psychology, Tokyo, 1971
Science and the Evolution of Consciousness: Chakras, Ki and Psi (with Rande Brown), Autumn Press, 1978

The above books are available from the Motoyama Institute – see address below. All other books listed here should be available from any bookshop.

Theories of the Chakras: Bridge to Higher Consciousness, Theosophical Publishing House, 1982
Toward a Superconsciousness: Meditational Theory and Practice, Asian Humanities Press (distributed in the UK by Element Books), 1990

For other information on Dr Motoyama's other English language publications (journals, monographs and scientific papers), teaching schedules and graduate school programmes, please contact:

Far East:
The Motoyama Institute for Life Physics, Inokashira 4-11-7, Mitak-shi, Tokyo 181, Japan

(Research Institute and teaching centre founded and directed by Dr Motoyama)

Americas:
The California Institute for Human Science, 701 Garden View Court, Encinitas, CA 92024, USA. Tel. 760 634 1771

(Graduate school and research centre founded by Dr Motoyama)

Europe:
Health Systems, PO Box 2211, Barnet, Herts, EN5 4QN, United Kingdom. Tel/Fax: 0181 449 7771

(European Representatives for Dr Motoyama)

INDEX

abortion, 17-18
Absolute, 2, 13, 41, 113, 128, 129, 136, 138
Ajna Chakra, 98
Amida Buddha, 128
Anahata Chakra, 98
ancestors, 52-8
animals, 26-7, 82
appetite, 30-1
Asana, 118
Asia, 109. 132-3
astral body, 11-13, 25, 88-91, 96-9, 124
astral dimension, 14-17, 82-3, 92-3, 95-6, 110, 143
astral energy, 69-70, 103-4
attachment: to desire, 30-1; to emotion, 31-5, 97; to knowledge, 98; to love, 98; to purification, 98; to self, 111-16; sexual, 30, 41-2, 48, 49, 97; to thought, 35-9
Avalokitesvara, 48

Bhagavad Gita, 92
birth, 17-22, 40, 102
birthmarks, 86, 95, 96
bonding, 41-51
brain, 121
breathing, 119-20, 123-4
Buddha, 94, 137
Buddhism, 29, 72, 85, 86, 94, 96, 114, 116, 122, 128, 132-3, 137, 138-9
Burma, 116

causal body, 11-13, 25, 96, 98-9, 126, 138
Causal Consciousness, 142-3, 145
causal dimension, 47, 82-3, 92, 95-6, 110
chakras, 11-12, 88, 89-91, 95-8
character, 105
children, 19-22, 26, 37, 52-4, 59-60, 105-6, 107
chimpanzees, 26
Chosaku, 111-16, 126, 127, 128, 143-4
Christianity, 28, 119-20, 132, 133, 134
clairvoyance, 87
Cleaner Wrasse, 50
communities, 109-10
concentration, 122-4
connections, 41
consciousness, 42, 125, 126, 137, 142-3, 145
crime, 105
cultural environment, 108-9

death, 22-4, 44-5, 75-6, 88-93, 141
depression, 33
desert religions, 131-2, 133-4
desire, attachment to, 30-1

dharana, 121-5
dissolving karma, 111-28
divinity, 110

Earth, global karma, 80-1, 130-1
Eckhart, Meister, 120
elderly people, 37-8
Eliade, Mircea, 125
emotions, 31-5, 36, 97
energy, 81; astral, 69-70, 103-4; centres, 11; ki, 69-70, 96, 118, 119
Enlightenment, 41, 138
Europeans, 109-10
evolution, 1, 2, 81-4
eyes, 121

family karma, 40-1, 51-60, 104, 106-7, 130
fantasy, 35-6
fate, 140-1
Feuerbach, Ludwig, 30
foetal spirits, 17-18
foetus, 105-6
forest religions, 131-5
Fujisawa Shojokoji, 114

genetics, 19, 106
geniuses, 37
geographic karma, 66-70, 104, 108, 130
Germany, 64
global karma, 80-1, 108, 130-1
God, 2, 12, 84, 113, 127-8, 132-3, 141
Greece, 70
group karma, 109-10
guardian angels, 25, 92

heredity, 19
Hinduism, 2, 70, 86, 116-26, 132, 138
Holy Spirit, 28
Homo Sapiens, 81
human beings, 24-7

ideation, 35-6
imagination, 35-8
India, 116
Indians, American, 63-4
infants, 37, 40-1
'instantaneous disintegration', 139-40
Islam, 132

Japan, 61-2, 64-6, 109
Jews, 66
Ji-sect, 114
Judaism, 132, 133

karma, 7-10; definition, 28-39; mechanism of manifestation, 99-110; storage of,